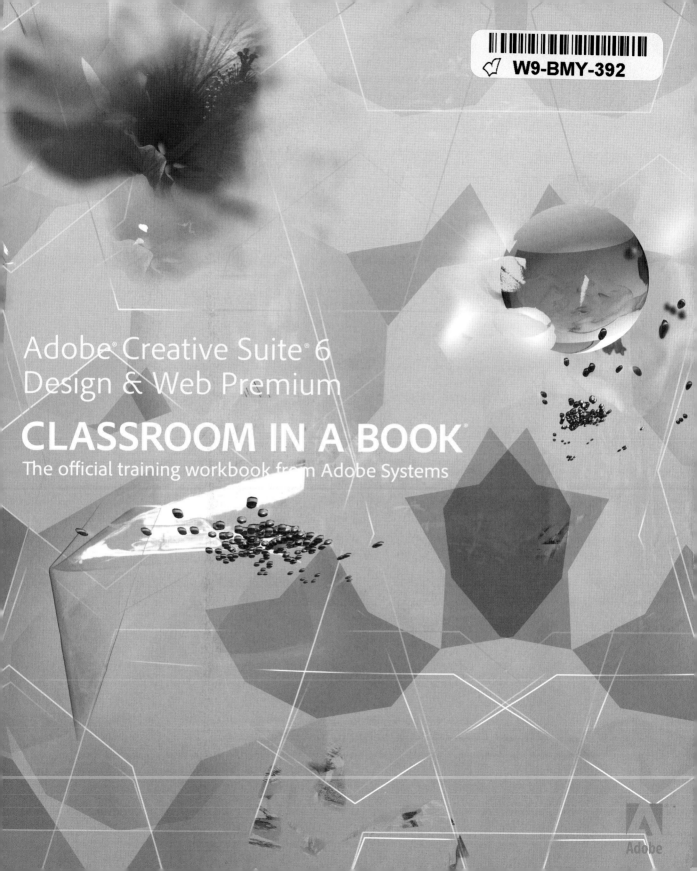

Adobe® Creative Suite® 6
Design & Web Premium

CLASSROOM IN A BOOK®

The official training workbook from Adobe Systems

Adobe

Adobe Press books are published by Peachpit, a division of Pearson Education located in Berkeley, California. For the latest on Adobe Press books, go to www.adobepress.com. To report errors, please send a note to errata@peachpit.com. For information on getting permission for reprints and excerpts, contact permissions@peachpit.com.

Writer: Conrad Chavez

Project Editor: Susan Rimerman

Production Editor: Tracey Croom

Development/Copyeditor: Anne Marie Walker

Technical Editor: Jean-Claude Tremblay

Proofer: Liz Welch

Compositor: Lisa Fridsma

Indexer: Rebecca Plunkett

Keystroker: David Van Ness

Cover design: Eddie Yuen

Interior design: Mimi Heft

Printed and bound in the United States of America

ISBN-13: 978-0-321-82260-4

ISBN-10: 0-321-82260-9

9 8 7 6 5 4 3 2 1

WHAT'S ON THE DISC

Here is an overview of the contents of the Classroom in a Book disc.

The *Adobe Creative Suite 6 Design & Web Premium Classroom in a Book* disc includes the lesson files that you'll need to complete the exercises in this book, as well as other content to help you learn more about Adobe Creative Suite 6 and use it with greater efficiency and ease. The diagram below represents the contents of the disc, which should help you locate the files you need.

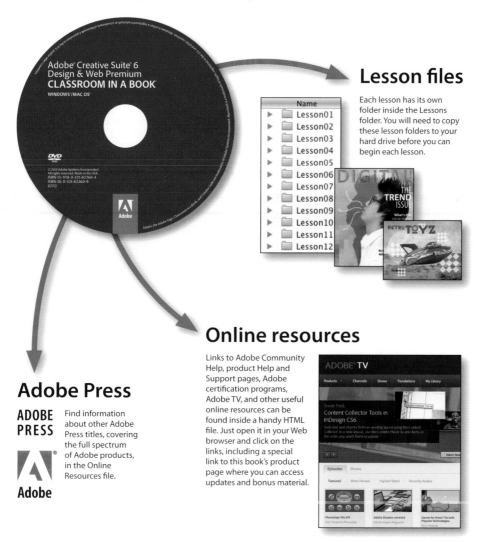

Lesson files

Each lesson has its own folder inside the Lessons folder. You will need to copy these lesson folders to your hard drive before you can begin each lesson.

Adobe Press

Find information about other Adobe Press titles, covering the full spectrum of Adobe products, in the Online Resources file.

Online resources

Links to Adobe Community Help, product Help and Support pages, Adobe certification programs, Adobe TV, and other useful online resources can be found inside a handy HTML file. Just open it in your Web browser and click on the links, including a special link to this book's product page where you can access updates and bonus material.

CONTENTS

GETTING STARTED

Adobe Creative Suite 6 Design & Web Premium is the ultimate toolkit for professional design. With it you can deliver eye-catching digital images and craft graphics that remain crisp when scaled. You can also lay out high-impact print pages with exquisite typography, build HTML5/CSS3 websites that look great on any screen, and design applications for tablets and smartphones.

This Classroom in a Book introduces you to the key elements and applications of Adobe Creative Suite 6 Design & Web Premium.

About Classroom in a Book

Adobe Creative Suite 6 Design & Web Premium Classroom in a Book is part of the official training series for Adobe graphics and publishing software developed with the support of Adobe product experts. Each lesson in this book is made up of a series of self-paced projects that give you hands-on experience using the following Adobe products: Adobe Photoshop CS6 Extended, Adobe Illustrator CS6, Adobe InDesign CS6, Adobe Dreamweaver CS6, Adobe Flash Professional CS6, Adobe Fireworks CS6, Adobe Acrobat X Pro, and Adobe Bridge CS6.

Adobe Creative Suite 6 Design & Web Premium Classroom in a Book includes a disc attached to the inside back cover. On the disc you'll find all the files used for the lessons in this book along with additional learning resources.

Prerequisites

Before you begin working on the lessons in this book, make sure that you and your computer are ready.

Computer requirements

You'll need about 1.07 GB of free space on your hard drive to store all of the lesson files and the work files that you'll create as you work through the exercises. You'll need less space if you don't store all of the lesson folders on your hard drive at once.

Required skills

The lessons in this book assume that you have a working knowledge of your computer and its operating system. Make sure that you know how to use the pointer and the standard menus and commands, and also how to open, save, and close files. You should also know how to use context menus, which open when you right-click/Ctrl-click items, and scroll (vertically and horizontally) within a window to see content that may not be visible in the displayed area.

If you need to review these basic and generic computer skills, see the documentation included with your Microsoft Windows or Apple Mac OS X software.

Installing Adobe Creative Suite 6 Design & Web Premium

Before you begin using *Adobe Creative Suite 6 Design & Web Premium Classroom in a Book*, make sure that your system is set up correctly and that you've installed the required software and hardware. You must purchase the Adobe Creative Suite 6 Design & Web Premium software separately. For system requirements and complete instructions on installing the software, see the Adobe Creative Suite 6 Design & Web Premium Read Me file on the application installation disc or the Adobe Creative Suite Support Center on the web at www.adobe.com/support/creativesuite.

Make sure that your serial number is accessible before installing the software; you can find the serial number on the registration card or disc sleeve. For software you downloaded as an electronic purchase directly from Adobe, look for your serial number in the order confirmation e-mail and in your Adobe Store account on Adobe.com.

Copying the Classroom in a Book files

The disc attached to the inside back cover of this book includes a Lessons folder containing all the files you'll need for the lessons. Each lesson has its own folder; you must copy the folders to your hard drive to complete the lessons. To save room on your hard drive, you can copy only the folder necessary for each lesson as you need it, and remove it when you're done.

Copying the lesson files from the disc

1　Insert the *Adobe Creative Suite 6 Design & Web Premium Classroom in a Book* disc into your optical disc drive.

2　Browse the contents and locate the Lessons folder.

3　Do one of the following:

- To copy all the lesson files, drag the Lessons folder from the disc onto your hard drive.

- To copy only individual lesson files, first create a new folder on your hard drive and name it Lessons. Then drag the lesson folder or folders that you want to copy from the disc into the Lessons folder on your hard drive.

4　When your computer has finished copying the files, remove the disc from your optical disc drive and put it away.

Additional Resources

Adobe Creative Suite 6 Design & Web Premium Classroom in a Book is not meant to replace documentation that comes with the program or to be a comprehensive reference for every feature. Only the commands and options used in the lessons are explained in this book. For comprehensive information about program features and tutorials, please refer to these resources:

Adobe Community Help: Community Help brings together active Adobe product users, Adobe product team members, authors, and experts to give you the most useful, relevant, and up-to-date information about Adobe products.

To access Community Help: To invoke Help, choose Help > [product name] Help. For example, in Photoshop, choose Help > Photoshop Help.

Adobe content is updated based on community feedback and contributions. You can add comments to both content or forums—including links to web content, publish your own content using Community Publishing, or contribute Cookbook Recipes. Find out how to contribute at www.adobe.com/community/publishing/download.html

See http://community.adobe.com/help/profile/faq.html for answers to frequently asked questions about Community Help.

Adobe Creative Suite Help and Support: www.adobe.com/support/creativesuite/ where you can find and browse Help and Support content on adobe.com.

Adobe Forums: http://forums.adobe.com lets you tap into peer-to-peer discussions, questions and answers on Adobe products.

Adobe TV: http://tv.adobe.com is an online video resource for expert instruction and inspiration about Adobe products, including a How To channel to get you started with your product.

Adobe Design Center: www.adobe.com/designcenter offers thoughtful articles on design and design issues, a gallery showcasing the work of top-notch designers, tutorials, and more.

Adobe Developer Connection: www.adobe.com/devnet is your source for technical articles, code samples, and how-to videos that cover Adobe developer products and technologies.

Resources for educators: www.adobe.com/education includes three free curriculums that use an integrated approach to teaching Adobe software and can be used to prepare for the Adobe Certified Associate exams.

Also check out these useful links:

Adobe Marketplace & Exchange: www.adobe.com/cfusion/exchange/ is a central resource for finding tools, services, extensions, code samples and more to supplement and extend your Adobe products.

Adobe Creative Suite 6 Design & Web Premium product home page: www.adobe.com/creativesuite/design.html

Adobe Labs: http://labs.adobe.com gives you access to early builds of cutting-edge technology, as well as forums where you can interact with both the Adobe development teams building that technology and other like-minded members of the community.

Adobe Certification

The Adobe training and certification programs are designed to help Adobe customers improve and promote their product-proficiency skills. There are four levels of certification:

- Adobe Certified Associate (ACA)
- Adobe Certified Expert (ACE)
- Adobe Certified Instructor (ACI)
- Adobe Authorized Training Center (AATC)

The Adobe Certified Associate (ACA) credential certifies that individuals have the entry-level skills to plan, design, build, and maintain effective communications using different forms of digital media.

The Adobe Certified Expert program is a way for expert users to upgrade their credentials. You can use Adobe certification as a catalyst for getting a raise, finding a job, or promoting your expertise.

If you are an ACE-level instructor, the Adobe Certified Instructor program takes your skills to the next level and gives you access to a wide range of Adobe resources.

Adobe Authorized Training Centers offer instructor-led courses and training on Adobe products, employing only Adobe Certified Instructors. A directory of AATCs is available at http://partners.adobe.com.

For information on the Adobe Certified programs, visit www.adobe.com/support/certification/main.html.

ADOBE CREATIVE SUITE 6 DESIGN & WEB PREMIUM

Deliver innovative ideas for print, web, tablets, and smartphones

Adobe Creative Suite 6 Design & Web Premium software is the ultimate design toolkit for creative freedom and precise control. With Design & Web Premium, you can deliver eye-catching digital images and craft illustrations and graphics that remain crisp when scaled; lay out high-impact print documents with exquisite typography; lay out publications for iPad and other tablet devices; build HTML5/CSS3 websites and applications that look great on any screen; and choose from among several tools to design compelling apps for delivery to tablets and smartphones via mobile marketplaces.

This overview begins by introducing you to Creative Suite 6 Design & Web Premium, discusses its key advantages, and then introduces the Adobe Creative Suite family.

The lessons in the rest of this book cover specific aspects of using the applications in much more detail.

As a designer, your job is to create content with impact—content that attracts, informs, inspires, and persuades. With Design & Web Premium, you can translate ambitious ideas into reality, moving smoothly and efficiently across multiple media.

The Ultimate Design Toolkit for Creative Freedom and Precise Control

The tools in Creative Suite 6 Design & Web Premium are best-of-class, optimized for performance and efficient workflow, and link to each other in ways that save you time and work. For example, Adobe InDesign CS6 can import your Adobe Photoshop CS6 document while preserving its layers, and Adobe Bridge serves as a hub and organizer for the images, video, text, and fonts you use throughout Design & Web Premium.

Adobe InDesign CS6

With deep roots in high-end print publishing, InDesign has evolved to provide powerful and precise layout features that you can use to meet the highest professional standards of creative design, typography, production, and final output. As a hub for publication design and production, InDesign is where everything comes together: With InDesign, you can lay out pages that include content, such as images from Adobe Photoshop CS6, scalable artwork from Adobe Illustrator CS6, and styled text from your word processor.

The highly sophisticated layout capabilities in InDesign now power digital publishing, from fast and efficient output of PDF files and EPUB ebooks, to the ability to work directly with Adobe Digital Publishing Suite to create book apps for tablets and smartphones. In Adobe InDesign CS6, Liquid Layout rules, Alternate Layouts, Linked Content, and Content Collector greatly simplify creating and maintaining layouts for multiple devices from one publication.

The new Liquid Layout feature in Adobe InDesign CS6 lets you define layout rules so you can design a layout once and have it adapt as you resize it to multiple page sizes, such as for tablets and other mobile devices.

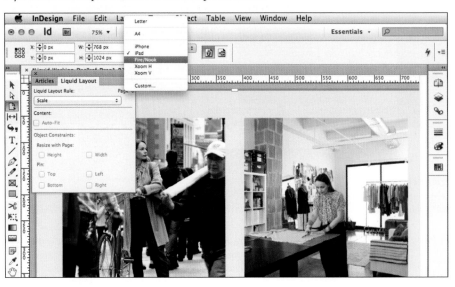

Adobe Dreamweaver CS6

With Adobe Dreamweave CS6 you can design, develop, and maintain standards-based websites and applications. The scope and power of Adobe Dreamweaver CS6 extends well beyond designing web pages. You can design to high visual standards using CSS3 and rich typography; manage pages, content, and code across an entire website; and ensure that your site is compatible with web standards and with a wide range of web browsers on desktop and laptop computers, tablets, and smartphones.

In a Dreamweaver project you can bring in content, such as images from Adobe Photoshop CS6, scalable artwork from Adobe Illustrator CS6, rich interactive content from Adobe Flash Professional CS6, and highly designed web graphics and layouts from Adobe Fireworks CS6.

In Adobe Dreamweaver CS6, development for modern web standards, such as HTML5 and CSS3, is made easier with features like Fluid Grid, which lets your layout adapt to different screen sizes.

Multiscreen Preview in Dreamweaver CS6 lets you preview how a web page layout looks on different mobile devices, and Fluid Grid lets the layout adapt to different page sizes.

Adobe Photoshop CS6 Extended

With Adobe Photoshop CS6 Extended, you can create powerful images with the standard in professional image editing software, and discover new dimensions in digital imaging. You can use Content-Aware retouching tools to greatly reduce the time it takes to correct and precisely retouch photographs for any medium, from print to online to mobile. You can also use intelligent editing tools to correct lens curvatures and other distortions, create photographic blur effects, straighten images in seconds, create 360-degree panoramas, extend depth of field, and more.

But Photoshop isn't just for photographs. You can design amazing graphics in the fewest number of steps using new and reengineered creative tools, and use type styles for consistent formatting, adjust the opacity and fill of multiple layers at once, blend images smoothly, and more.

Now that it's easier to create motion and 3D content, you can use Photoshop CS6 Extended to work with video and 3D elements; easily create rich 3D artwork with shadows, lighting, and animation; create vibrant videos and design anything you can imagine using intuitive tools; and get blazingly fast performance with the Monaco Graphics Engine.

Tilt-Shift Blur simulates shallow depth of field in Adobe Photoshop CS6 using intuitive new on-image controls.

Adobe Illustrator CS6

With Adobe Illustrator CS6, you can express your vision with shapes, color, effects, and typography. Adobe Illustrator CS6 software is the industry's premier vector-drawing environment for creating graphics that scale across media. You can work efficiently and move easily among Adobe applications and experiment freely with perspective, image tracing, transparent gradients, patterns, brushes, and strokes, which are all driven by the Venus Performance System so you can make fast work of your most complex designs.

Create your artwork in Adobe Illustrator when you want to draw smooth curves and logos that stay sharp when scaled to any size, detailed linework, information graphics, and symbol-based artwork and patterns that you can easily update.

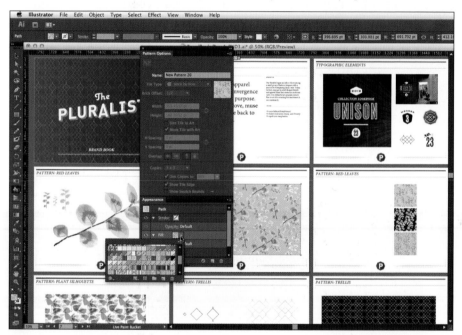

Design seamless patterns intuitively with new tools in Adobe Illustrator CS6, and view your artwork more quickly with the Venus Performance System.

Adobe Flash Professional CS6

Create and deliver rich, engaging experiences across devices with Adobe Flash Professional CS6, which is powerful authoring software for creating animation and multimedia content. With pixel-precise drawing and animation tools, professional typography, efficient coding features, high-quality video, and sprite-sheet generation, you can deliver immersive interactive experiences that can display consistently to audiences practically anywhere.

Export symbols and animation sequences from Adobe Flash Professional CS6 to instantly generate sprite sheets that improve gaming experience, workflow, and performance.

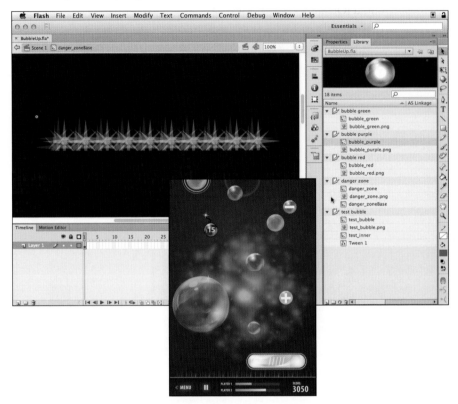

Adobe Fireworks CS6

Create beautiful designs for websites and mobile apps, all without coding and in a snap, with Adobe Fireworks CS6 software. You can deliver vector and bitmap images, mockups, 3D graphics, and interactive content for popular tablets and smartphones. You can optimize graphics and web content to display consistently across devices, and jump-start your designs with templates, rich symbols, and CSS sprites. In addition, you can smooth the workflow between design and coding with CSS extraction and jQuery Mobile themes.

Adobe Fireworks CS6 is optimized for designing visually compelling websites and mobile apps quickly and without coding.

Adobe Acrobat X Pro

With Adobe Acrobat X Pro, you can create and edit professional PDF files that can include rich media, share information securely, and manage document reviews efficiently. If you design print publications, PDF is a standard format for delivering print jobs to press, and for this reason, Acrobat X Pro integrates smoothly with Adobe InDesign CS6.

PDF is also a standard format for sharing documents online. You can design interactive forms, protect sensitive information, add media such as video and audio, and include multiple materials in one file. You can also organize and track online reviews of shared documents and collect comments.

With Acrobat X Pro, you can create professional PDF documents that are easy to share online. Acrobat is also an effective way to manage shared document reviews and feedback.

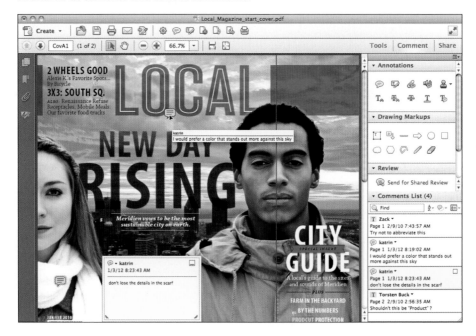

Adobe Bridge CS6

With Adobe Bridge CS6, you can manage your media with centralized access to all of your creative assets. Regardless of the Adobe Creative Suite software you use, your projects will likely involve various files and formats. You may be organizing documents and graphics from different sources or finding your way through a large media library. Adobe Bridge is a powerful media manager that helps you quickly locate and organize the files you need, and move them directly into the Adobe Creative Suite software you're using. Bridge helps you work with images, text, the native file formats of Creative Suite software—such as Photoshop, InDesign, and Illustrator—videos, fonts, and more. Powerful searching, content filters, and thumbnail views help you home in on the files you need, and large previews let you ensure that you're opening the correct file. Use the Output panel to batch-process files to PDF contact sheets, HTML web galleries, and more; and to upload images to online services such as Flickr and Facebook.

Stay organized by using Adobe Bridge CS6 to quickly locate, identify, and collect the files you use in Adobe Creative Suite projects. You can also apply keywords and metadata to photographs in bulk.

Keep Pace With Today's Media

Adobe has continually worked to keep Adobe Creative Suite in step with the latest standards and audiences. Adobe Creative Suite 6 Design & Web Premium includes essential performance and workflow enhancements, and brings you the tools you need to efficiently create HTML5/CSS3 media for new platforms, such as smartphones and tablets, while maintaining a professional level of control and precision.

Enjoy blazing-fast image editing and illustration

Adobe Creative Suite 6 Design & Web Premium features performance enhancements in several tools so you can deliver your best ideas at astonishing speed and take advantage of today's computer hardware. You can also work with large, complex files and apply creative effects, such as blurs, glows, and drop shadows, without missing a beat.

You'll work more quickly for two reasons: faster software and more efficient workflows. Key tools, such as Photoshop CS6, Illustrator CS6, Dreamweaver CS6, and Bridge CS6, are optimized for 64-bit hardware and contain performance enhancements that get the most out of today's systems. More efficient workflows include the Content-Aware tools that save you hours of manual retouching in Photoshop CS6, and easy pattern creation and accurate image tracing in Illustrator CS6.

Expand your design repertoire

With Design & Web Premium, you can break new creative ground without learning new software; take advantage of the 3D and video tools in Photoshop Extended to extend your portfolio beyond 2D still images; and go beyond print by creating highly designed ebooks and media-rich publications for iPad and other tablet devices in InDesign. Versatile preview options in Dreamweaver, Fireworks, and InDesign make it easier to see how your work will look on different screens.

Leverage essential tools for web design

You can craft layouts that respond to any screen by building HTML5/CSS3 websites in Dreamweaver. Dreamweaver also offers support for the latest HTML5/CSS3 standards and frameworks, including jQuery Mobile, PhoneGap, and WebKit.

The Adobe Creative Suite 6 Family

Adobe Creative Suite 6 Design & Web Premium is part of the Adobe Creative Suite 6 Family. This range of breakthrough interactive design tools enables you to create, deliver, and optimize beautiful, high-impact digital experiences across media and devices; create once and deliver that same experience virtually everywhere thanks to the ability to create a wide range of output, including web standard format, PDF, and Flash; and maximize the impact of what you've created through integration with SiteCatalyst and the Adobe Online Marketing Suite. You can choose from several editions of Adobe Creative Suite 6 to meet your specific needs.

Adobe Creative Suite 6 Design & Web Premium

Adobe Creative Suite 6 Design & Web Premium software is the ultimate toolkit for designers who need to express their wildest ideas with precision; work fluidly across media; and produce exceptional results in print, web, interactive, and mobile design. Craft eye-catching images and graphics, lay out stunning pages, build standards-based websites, create interactive content without writing code, and extend page layouts for viewing with ebook reading devices.

Adobe Creative Suite 6 Design & Web Premium software offers a host of productivity features for print design, including more precise image selection in Adobe Photoshop, enhanced object editing in Adobe InDesign, and perspective drawing in Adobe Illustrator. Revolutionize everyday creative work with innovative painting tools in Photoshop and Illustrator.

Design & Web Premium combines full new versions of InDesign CS6, Illustrator CS6, Photoshop CS6 Extended, Flash Professional CS6, Dreamweaver CS6, Fireworks CS6, and Acrobat X Pro, and Adobe Bridge CS6.

Adobe Creative Suite 6 Design Standard

For design and production professionals focused on print publishing who do not need the full-fledged web, interactive, and mobile design capabilities of Dreamweaver, Flash, and Fireworks, or the advanced video, animation, and 3D editing tools in Photoshop Extended, Adobe offers Adobe Creative Suite 6 Design Standard software.

Adobe Creative Suite 6 Production Premium

Conquer today's deadlines and tomorrow's challenges with Adobe Creative Suite 6 Production Premium software, the ultimate video production toolkit. Craft video productions, motion graphics, visual effects, and interactive experiences with high-performance, industry-leading creative tools. Boost your productivity with tightly integrated components that deliver breakthrough performance and smooth production workflows, giving you the power to produce engaging media for virtually any screen.

With the latest versions of Adobe's best-of-breed video, audio, and design tools, CS6 Production Premium offers enhancements that help you work more efficiently when tackling a broad spectrum of planning, production, and postproduction tasks. Each component offers a familiar user interface and integrates with other components for a complete, end-to-end toolset that accelerates video editing workflows from scriptwriting through postproduction.

For motion graphic designers and visual effects artists, CS6 Production Premium offers best-of-breed video, animation, compositing, audio, and design tools that feel like a natural extension of your creative process. Work more efficiently with high-resolution projects and benefit from tight integration between Adobe Photoshop Extended, Illustrator, and Adobe Premiere Pro.

Production Premium combines full new versions of Premiere Pro CS6, After Effects CS6, Photoshop CS6 Extended, Illustrator CS6, Flash Professional CS6, Adobe Audition CS6, and Encore CS6, and with Adobe Bridge CS6 and Dynamic Link.

Adobe Creative Suite 6 Master Collection

Tell your story from start to finish with one comprehensive offering. Adobe Creative Suite 6 Master Collection software enables you to design and develop amazing work, collaborate effectively, and deliver virtually anywhere.

With this software package, you can craft a corporate identity using Illustrator CS6 to engage your audience online, extending your creative reach. Design and deliver immersive experiences. Use Flash Professional CS6 to engage your audience with microsites and casual games that present your designs consistently across desktops, browsers, and mobile devices.

Take your story to any screen. Enhance HD video productions with high-resolution imagery from Photoshop CS6 Extended. Add intricate effects using After Effects CS6, and edit dramatically faster in Adobe Premiere Pro CS6.

Master Collection combines full new versions of Photoshop CS6 Extended, Illustrator CS6, InDesign CS6, Acrobat X Pro, Flash Professional CS6, Flash Builder 4, Dreamweaver CS6, Fireworks CS6, Premiere Pro CS6, After Effects CS6, Adobe Audition CS6, Encore CS6, Adobe Bridge CS6, Adobe Prelude CS6, and Dynamic Link.

Common features

No matter which edition of Creative Suite 6 you choose, you gain a toolset with integration that's enhanced by the following:

Adobe Bridge CS6 software is a powerful media manager that provides centralized access to all your creative assets.

In Production Premium CS6 and Master Collection, Adobe Dynamic Link gives you tighter-than-ever integration when moving assets between Adobe After Effects CS6, Adobe Premiere Pro CS6, and Encore CS6. An integral part of Adobe Creative Suite 6 Production Premium and Master Collection software, Dynamic Link enables you to work faster and stay in the creative flow by eliminating intermediate rendering when you make changes to assets—whether you're editing a sequence of clips in Adobe Premiere Pro, changing a composition in After Effects, or refining a project in Encore.

Adobe Creative Cloud

Adobe® Creative Cloud™ is a creative hub where you can explore, create, publish, and share your work using Adobe Creative Suite desktop applications, Adobe Touch Apps, and services together for a complete idea-to-publishing experience. Adobe Creative Cloud turns previously difficult, disparate workflows into one intuitive, natural experience, allowing you to create freely and deliver ideas on any desktop, tablet, or handheld device.

Adobe Creative Cloud is an optional membership that isn't just about online services. It provides you with all of the Adobe Creative Suite desktop applications (the Master Collection), as well as the Adobe Touch Apps for mobile devices, and a set of online services such as cloud storage for your files, device sync, and Adobe Typekit web-based fonts. Adobe Creative Cloud also provides the latest versions of the tools you rely on, so that you can easily stay up-to-date with the constant, rapid changes in the industry.

At the time this book was published, Adobe Creative Cloud was being prepared for its initial release. For the latest information about Adobe Creative Cloud, visit http://www.adobe.com/products/creativecloud.html.

1 SETTING UP BASIC ASSETS

Lesson Overview

The way you set up your documents and create your assets will affect how easily and efficiently you can design your work. This lesson will introduce you to some important skills and concepts:

- Organizing your work in Adobe Bridge
- Automatically tracing an image in Illustrator
- Drawing expressively with the Bristle Brush in Illustrator
- Creating a pattern in Illustrator
- Refining a vector graphic in Illustrator with the Blob Brush tool
- Setting up multiple Illustrator artboards for design variations
- Drawing in perspective in Illustrator
- Cropping a photo in Photoshop Extended
- Removing a background in Photoshop Extended
- Removing unwanted objects in Photoshop Extended
- Moving objects seamlessly in Photoshop Extended
- Adding creative blur in Photoshop Extended

 You'll probably need between one and two hours to complete this lesson.

In this lesson, you'll be working on exciting projects: turning a hand sketch into a pattern, creating expressive artwork, and getting photos ready for a layout. You'll be preparing assets that you'll use in a printed and interactive brochure in lessons later in this book.

Organizing Your Work with Adobe Bridge

In this lesson, you'll set up some of the basic assets that you'll use for projects in this book. You'll be working in Adobe Bridge, Adobe Illustrator, Adobe Photoshop Extended, and Adobe Acrobat.

Adobe Bridge CS6 provides integrated, centralized access to your project files and enables you to quickly browse through your creative assets visually—regardless of what format they're in—making it easy for you to locate, organize, and view your files.

Adding folders to your Favorites

To help you access your files easily, Adobe Bridge adds your Pictures and Documents folders (Mac) or your My Pictures and My Documents folders (Windows) to the Favorites panel by default. You can add as many of your frequently used applications, folders, and documents as you like. In the Preferences dialog box for Adobe Bridge you can even specify which of the default favorites you want to keep in the Favorites panel.

After you've copied the Lessons folder from the *Adobe Creative Suite 6 Classroom in a Book* disc to your hard drive, it's a good idea to add your Lessons folder to the Favorites panel in Adobe Bridge, so that the files you'll use for the lessons in this book will be only a click away. You could add your Lesson01 folder right below that and keep it there while you work through this lesson.

1 Start Adobe Bridge CS6. At the top of the Adobe Bridge browser window, make sure the Essentials workspace is selected.

2 Navigate to your Lessons folder, and then select the Lesson01 folder in the Content panel. Drag it into the Favorites panel in the left panel group and drop it under the Pictures folder.

Having your Lessons files easily accessible, will save you a great deal of time as you work your way through the lessons in this book.

Adding metadata

All your documents contain some metadata, such as information about the device with which they were created. You can use Adobe Bridge to add your own metadata to a single file or to multiple files at the same time—without having to open the application specific to those files.

In this first exercise you'll see how easy it is to add metadata to a file and learn some different ways to mark it, which will make it easier to find and sort.

1   In Adobe Bridge, navigate to your Lesson01 folder to see the files inside. You'll be working with these files later in this lesson.

2   Select the file Adobe_0367.tif and note the Metadata panel in the right panel group.

3   In the Metadata panel, expand the IPTC Core panel, and type **pink, dress** in the Keywords text field.

▶ **Tip:** If you can't read all your filenames or the thumbnail images are not big enough, you can enlarge them by using the Zoom slider in the lower-right corner.

What you just did is enter two keywords, using a comma to separate them so they are entered individually. You can also enter keywords using the Keywords panel that you may see grouped with the Metadata panel, but when you're entering many types of metadata, you may find it more convenient to enter them in the Metadata panel along with everything else.

4   Press Enter/Return to apply your entries.

When you search for this file in the future, the metadata you just added will help you to find this specific file. Adobe Bridge looks in the metadata fields when you search for a file in Adobe Bridge, and in addition, the search features built into Microsoft Windows and Mac OS X also look for keywords to improve their search results.

▶ **Tip:** Keywords you enter are searchable in the search field in the top-right corner of an Adobe Bridge window, as well as in Mac OS X Spotlight and Windows Desktop Search. They can also be preserved when exporting versions of the images to share online.

Marking your files with ratings and color labels

When you're working with a large number of files and folders, assigning ratings and labels is a good way to mark a large number of files quickly, making it easier to sort and find them later.

1   In the Content menu, note the five dots above the filename Adobe_0367.tif, indicating that this file has not yet been rated. Click on the third dot, which will apply a three-star rating—it's that easy to rate a file.

You can also mark a file visually by assigning a color label.

2   Choose Label > Approved. Your file is marked with a green color label, which you can also see in the right panel group.

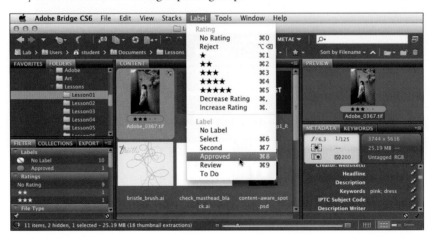

About Image Trace

A lot of great design ideas start out as a great pencil sketch on paper. To keep the precious spontaneity of such hand-drawn scribbles, it's best to bring the graphics straight into Illustrator and trace them. Placing a scanned file into Illustrator and automatically tracing the artwork with the Image Trace command is the easiest way to do so. The illustrations below show studies for a logo.

Image Trace automatically turns placed images into detailed vector graphics that are easy to edit, resize, and manipulate without distortion. And, as Illustrator fans know already, Image Trace enables you to produce stunning-looking illustrations by changing rasterized images into vector-based drawings. You'll appreciate how quickly you can re-create a scanned drawing onscreen, maintaining its quality and authentic feel.

This color labeling system is not only useful to help you quickly spot the images you're looking for, but is also an effective way to sort your images by category, production status, or any other meanings you assign to the labels. This can be a useful organizational tool, especially when different people are working on the same project. You can use the Filter panel to quickly locate files with specific ratings or labels.

3 Right-click / Control-click the image of the woman again, and this time choose Sort > By Label from the context menu. If you had multiple files with the same label, they would now be grouped in the Content panel. You can change the sort order by toggling View > Sort > Ascending Order.

Synchronizing color management

Using Adobe Bridge as your central hub enables you to synchronize the color management settings across all your Creative Suite applications. It's highly recommended to use this feature so that the colors in your images will look the same regardless of which Creative Suite component application you're working with.

There are a range of options for synchronizing color management. You can specify your own color settings in the Color Settings dialog box in the relevant Adobe application, and then apply it to all the other Adobe Creative Suite applications in Adobe Bridge, or you can choose one of the Adobe Bridge presets.

1   In Adobe Bridge, choose Edit > Creative Suite Color Settings.

2   The Suite Color Settings dialog box appears. A message at the top of the dialog box tells you whether or not the settings are already synchronized. If they are not, choose North America General Purpose 2 from the Color Settings menu, and then click Apply. If the Apply button isn't active, select any setting, and then select North America General Purpose 2 and click Apply.

The next time you open the Suite Color Settings dialog box, the message at the top of the Suite Color Settings dialog box should now indicate that all your CS6 applications use the same color management settings.

Creating Artwork in Illustrator

When you're designing graphics such as logos and corporate identities, it's an absolute must that your design be scalable, because the graphic will be used in a wide range of applications, from web pages at screen resolution to high-resolution printed matter or even monumental signage. For designing graphics that need to be resolution independent, Adobe Illustrator is the world's leading vector-based application. Today, other applications in the Creative Suite, such as InDesign and Photoshop, also let you create vector graphics using the Pen tool (among others); however, your best choice is still Illustrator, because it includes the most comprehensive set of drawing tools.

Bitmap versus vector graphics

Pixel- or raster-based applications, such as Photoshop, are unbeatable when it comes to producing photographic or continuous-tone images. However, these images are composed of a fixed number of pixels, resulting in a jagged—or pixelated—look when they are enlarged. The illustration below clearly shows the difference between a resolution-independent vector graphic (left) and a pixel-based graphic (right).

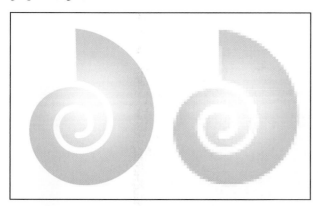

With Illustrator, you create vector graphics—artwork that is made up of points, lines, and curves that are expressed as mathematical vectors. Vector-based graphics are resolution independent—they can be scaled to any size without losing quality or crispness.

Automatically trace an image as a vector graphic with Image Trace in Illustrator

There are times when the job calls for a smooth, scalable vector graphic, such as a logo, but you have a bitmap graphic. Image Trace in Illustrator makes it easy to convert a bitmap graphic to a vector graphic by accurately following its contours and edges.

You'll trace a scan of a hand-sketched idea, and later you'll use the traced image as the basis for a pattern.

1 In Illustrator, choose File > New, click the Landscape icon, leave the rest of the settings as they are, and click OK.

2 Arrange the Adobe Bridge window for your Lesson01 folder and the Illustrator document window so that you can see both at the same time.

3 Drag the file diagram013.jpg from the Lesson01 folder in Adobe Bridge, and drop it in the middle of the Illustrator document window; after dragging, you can enlarge the Illustrator document window.

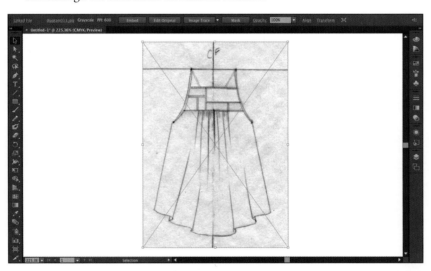

4 Click the Zoom tool (🔍), and drag a rectangle around the scan to make the scan fill the document window.

5 In the Control panel, click Image Trace. If a tracing warning appears, click Cancel.

Illustrator warns you if an image is so large that it may take a long time to trace and suggests downsampling the image to a lower resolution. Because this 600 ppi image is a rough sketch, 600 ppi is not necessary, so you'll resample it to a quarter of that resolution.

6 Choose Object > Rasterize, choose Medium (150 ppi) from the Resolution pop-up menu, and click OK.

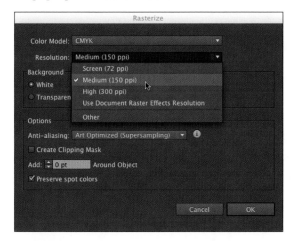

7 In the Control panel, click Image Trace.

8 With the Zoom tool, zoom into a detail of the sketch. You'll see that it's a set of smooth vector shapes. The bitmapped gray tones of the original sketch image were interpreted by Image Trace as sharp, smooth vector paths, replacing the "jaggies" of the pixels of the original bitmap image.

> ▶ **Tip:** To see the pixels of the original untraced graphic, you can choose Source Image from the View pop-up menu in the Control panel as long as the tracing results have not been expanded.

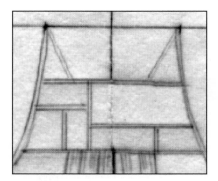

Original scan of sketch   Tracing result

Because the traced graphic is selected, you can see Image Tracing options in the Control panel across the top of the workspace.

9 In the Options bar, click the Image Trace panel button to see more options that determine the tracing result.

10 In the Image Trace panel, if the Preset pop-up menu doesn't display Sketched Art, choose it, and make sure the Preview check box is selected. When Preview is not selected, you must click Trace to update the tracing result.

> ▶ **Tip:** In the Image Trace panel, the Preview check box redraws the tracing result as soon as you change options. If you don't want to wait for screen redraw before changing additional options, deselect the Preview check box.

The Sketched Art preset allows the traced object to have a transparent background by ignoring white areas. This will be important when you use this tracing as the basis for a pattern over a colored background.

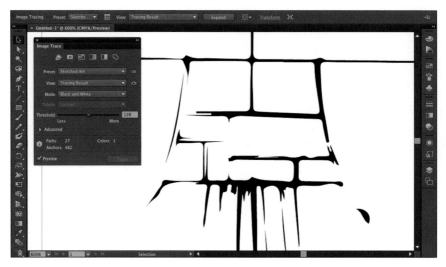

11 In the Image Trace panel, drag the Threshold slider to the right. The line quality of the tracing becomes heavier, because it's including darker tones of the image in the trace result.

12 Set the slider to **160** to give the trace a loosely sketched look.

13 Close the Image Trace panel, and zoom out until you can see the entire traced sketch with a little space around it.

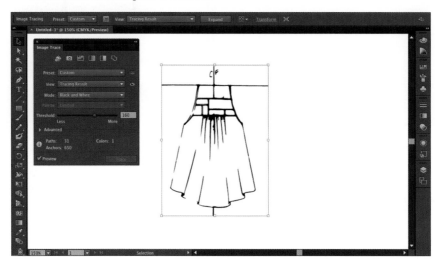

14 Choose File > Save As, name the file **Sketch.ai**, and save it into your Lesson01 folder. When the Illustrator Options dialog box appears, click OK to accept the default settings. Leave the document open for the next section.

Because Image Trace is nondestructive, it retains the original image so you can always start over. Although you could use the graphic as is, in the next section you'll apply some additional processing so you can use it as a pattern.

Creating a pattern

The Pattern Options panel, new in Adobe Illustrator CS6, makes it easy to quickly create patterns by creative experimentation. You'll start with the traced graphic you just created. You can't directly colorize a traced object, so you'll expand it into paths.

1 If the traced graphic isn't still selected, click it with the Selection tool.

2 In the Control panel, click Expand.

3 Choose Object > Path > Clean Up, make sure all three options are selected, and click OK. This removes redundant paths generated as a by-product of Image Trace, leaving a simpler graphic that's easier to color.

4 Click the Fill swatch in the Tools panel, and in the Swatches panel, click a red swatch.

5 Choose Select > Deselect to see how the colored graphic looks now, and then choose File > Save.

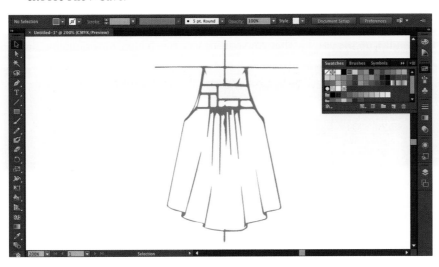

6 Use the Selection tool to select the graphic again, and then choose Object > Pattern > Make. If an alert appears telling you that the new pattern has been added to the Swatches panel, click OK.

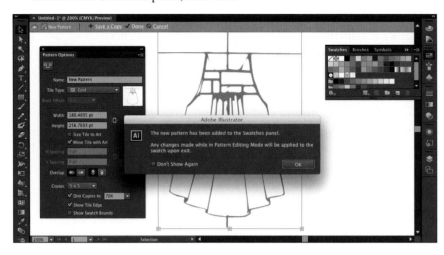

Creating the pattern changes the the document window. There's now a gray bar at the top of the document window, which indicates that you've entered Pattern Editing mode. Because you're in Pattern Editing mode, the graphic now repeats throughout the document window so that you can preview the pattern as you edit it.

7 Zoom out to see more of the pattern preview.

▶ **Tip:** You can name a pattern by typing into the Name option at the top of the Pattern Options panel.

8 In the Pattern Options panel, click the Pattern Tile tool (▣), and use it to drag the handles on the graphic that you're using as a tile. Notice how dragging the handles controls the spacing between pattern tiles.

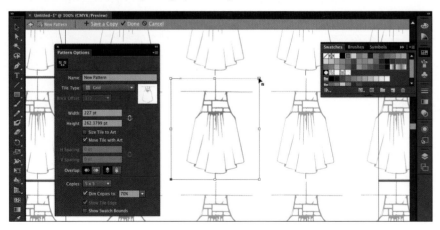

9 With the Rectangle tool, draw a rectangle that matches the pattern tile size. The green Smart Guides help you snap exactly to the pattern tile edges and corners.

10 Click the peach-colored swatch at the top-right corner of the Swatches panel, and then choose Object > Arrange > Send to Back. If there's a white gap along any side of the pattern tile, adjust the peach-filled rectangle as needed to create a solid background for the pattern.

11 With the rectangle still selected, choose Object > Lock > Selection.

▶ **Tip:** When you edit a pattern, the gray bar at the top of a document window indicates an *isolation mode*—a way that Illustrator lets you edit components of an illustration such as groups, patterns, and symbols without risking accidental changes to other parts of the document.

12 Choose Select > Select All, and then choose Object > Group.

13 With the Selection tool, Alt-drag / Option-drag the sketch to the left to create a copy, and center it over the left edge of the pattern tile.

14 Alt-drag / Option-drag a corner handle of the sketch copy to proportionally scale it down until it's about a third of the size of the original.

15 If only half of the sketch repeats, click the Left in Front or Right in Front button in the Pattern Options panel until it looks right.

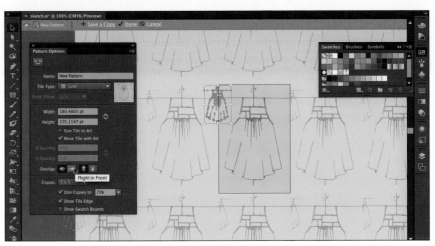

16 In the Tile Type pop-up in the Pattern Options panel, select the Brick by Row and Brick by Column options and observe how they change the pattern offset. Choose the one you like the most. (The Hex by Column and Hex by Row options work properly only with hexagonal pattern tiles.)

17 Choose Select > Deselect.

18 Select the Brush tool, click a yellow swatch in the Swatches panel, and then in the Control panel change the Opacity to 50%. Paint strokes of color into the pattern. To seamlessly tile brush strokes that overlap the tile edge, cross over the same side as the smaller version of the sketch, because that's the Overlap side you specified in the Pattern Options panel earlier.

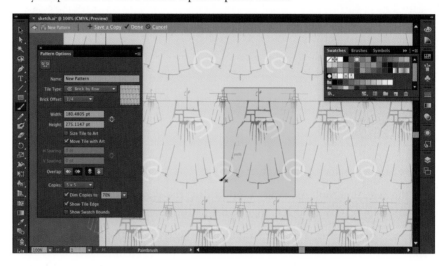

The pattern is now ready, so it's time to leave Pattern Editing mode.

19 In the Pattern Editing mode bar at the top of the document, click Done. If an alert appears, click OK.

Do not be alarmed when the pattern disappears. It's saved in the pattern swatch that was created in the Swatches panel when you originally created the new pattern. Now you'll use the pattern.

20 With the Selection tool, select the traced dress and press the Delete key. After creating a pattern from this graphic, you no longer need it.

21 With the Rectangle tool, drag a rectangle that's roughly the same size as the page.

22 Click the pattern swatch you created, to apply it to the rectangle. Resize the rectangle to see how the pattern automatically tiles within the object.

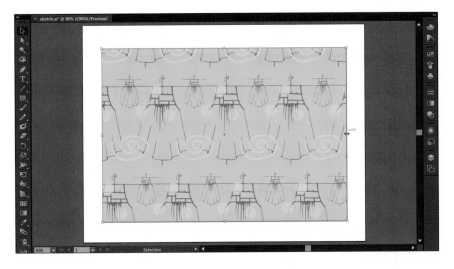

23 With the pattern-filled object selected, choose Object > Pattern > Edit Pattern. The document enters Pattern Editing mode, which you can recognize because of the tiled preview and the gray Pattern Editing mode bar at the top of the document window. Click Done to leave Pattern Editing mode, or press Esc.

24 Close the document, saving changes if asked.

Congratulations! You've learned how to create, apply, and edit a pattern. You can now use it to illustrate textiles, interiors, or other designs.

Creating a vector graphic with the Bristle Brush

You don't need to use a painting program to create expressive brush strokes. In Illustrator CS6, the Bristle Brush gives you the creative possibilities of traditional media like watercolors, oils, and pastels while also providing the speed, editability, and scalability you expect with vector graphics. If you have a Wacom tablet, you can control Bristle Brush strokes with stylus pressure, and with Wacom Intous tablets you can also control strokes using tilt angle, bearing, and barrel rotation.

1 In your Lesson01 folder in Adobe Bridge, double-click the file bristle_brush.ai.

2 In the Layers panel, make the Model layer visible by clicking to show the eye icon for that layer.

3 With the Selection tool, select the pink dress.

4 In the Tools panel, click the Drawing Modes icon () and choose Draw Inside. This will let you draw freely and keep your artwork inside the dress.

5 Choose Select > Deselect, and then select the Brush tool.

6 Choose Window > Brushes, and then choose New Brush from the Brushes panel menu. In the New Brush dialog box, select Bristle Brush and click OK.

7 In the Bristle Brush Options dialog box, choose Round Point from the Shape menu. Change the Size to 10mm, and then click OK to close the dialog box.

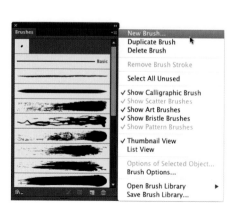

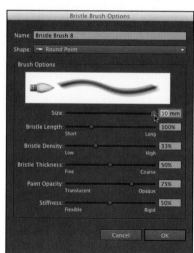

8 In the Tools panel, make sure Stroke color is active, and then in the Swatches panel, select a color that's different than the dress.

9 Drag the brush inside the dress to paint with broad strokes. Try different colors.

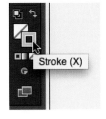

10 With the Selection tool, select the tallest pink swirl behind the model.

11 In the Brushes panel, select the 4.80mm round fan brush named Bristle Brush 6. Notice how the swirl now appears as if it had been painted freehand. In this way, you can easily apply Bristle Brush strokes to a path you've already drawn. Feel free to apply other brushes to the remaining swirls.

12 Choose File > Save As, navigate to your Lesson01 folder, name the file **bristle_brush_done.ai**, and click Save. If warning alerts appear, click OK to close each of them.

13 Close the document.

Refining a vector graphic with the Blob Brush tool

If you have been working with the brushes in Flash and Photoshop, you'll find similarities in the Blob Brush in Illustrator, which enables you to generate a clean vector shape as you paint. Used in combination with the Eraser tool, the Blob Brush provides a truly painterly, intuitive way to create vector shapes—merging your brush strokes into a single, fluid outline that can then be filled with a solid color or painted with a gradient or even a pattern.

In this exercise you'll design a variation on an existing graphic by refining the outline of a masthead logo that was traced from handwritten artwork using Image Trace in Illustrator.

1 In your Lesson01 folder in Adobe Bridge, double-click the file check_masthead_black.ai.

Blob Brush tool —

Eyedropper —

Zoom tool —

2 In Illustrator, select the Zoom tool in the Tools panel, or press the Z key, and then click to zoom in close enough to scrutinize the outline of the logo in detail. Some of the unevenness you see along the edges can be smoothed out with the Blob Brush tool.

3 Before using the brush, first make sure the correct color for the check logo is active. The logo is filled with black and has no stroke. Select the Eyedropper tool in the Tools panel and click on the logo. The Color panel will display a black fill and no stroke.

4 In the Tools panel, double-click the Blob Brush tool. Make sure that the Fidelity slider is set to 3 pixels, and that brush Size is set to 3 pt in the Default Brush Options. Then click OK.

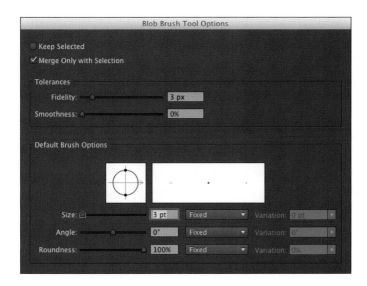

5 To demonstrate the refinements possible with the Blob Brush, let's have a closer look at the letter *e* in the check logo. Notice the dent in the lower-left side. With the Blob Brush still selected, add a few strokes to smooth the outline.

6 If you are not happy with the strokes you just painted with the Blob Brush tool, use the Eraser tool in the Tools panel to correct them—the Eraser tool edits your strokes while maintaining them as filled vector paths.

7 When you're happy with your refinements to the logo, select the Zoom tool (🔍), press the Alt/Option key for the Zoom Out mode, and then click on the logo to zoom out until you can see the entire document.

8 Choose File > Save As, navigate to your Lesson01 folder, name the file **check_masthead_done.ai**, and click Save; if the Illustrator Options dialog box appears, click OK. Then close the document.

Next, you'll take advantage of another great feature of Illustrator CS6: multiple artboards, which are like separate pages within one file. You'll create another artboard for a copy of the logo.

Working with multiple artboards

● **Note:** When you create a new Illustrator document, you can specify the number of artboards you want and their size, position, and spacing in the New Document dialog box.

In Illustrator CS6, you can work with up to 100 different artboards in a single file. You can control the size of the artboards as well as the spacing in between them. Multiple artboards can be named and organized in rows and columns, and can be printed, exported, and saved separately.

Being able to have several artboards within one file suits the way most designers work: Usually, numerous iterations of a design concept are necessary to arrive at the polished final version. To help you create variations, you can quickly copy an object across all artboards.

1   In your Lesson01 folder, open the file AI_Artboards.ai.

This file contains four artboards in a horizontal row. You may not be able to see them all right away.

2   Choose View > Fit All in Window. Now you can see all artboards at once.

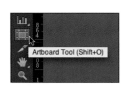

3   Select the Artboard tool, and click the second artboard to select it.

The Control panel updates to present artboard options; this is where you can set the size, orientation, and name of the selected artboard.

You can freely arrange artboards; they don't have to be perfectly aligned. In this case, the four artboards will fit better on the screen if arranged as two rows.

4 Under the View menu, make sure Smart Guides is selected. As you drag, green Smart Guides appear to indicate exact alignment of edges and centers.

5 Using the Artboard tool, drag the third artboard until it's under the first artboard and the green centering Smart Guide appears.

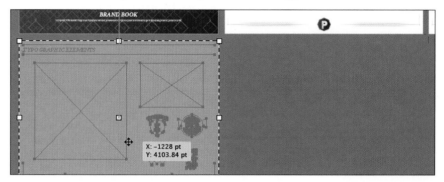

6 Drag the fourth artboard until it's under the second artboard, and the green centering Smart Guide appears to indicate alignment with the artboards above and to the left.

7 Choose View > Fit All in Window to fit the new arrangement of artboards into the document window.

When you use multiple artboards, you may want to include common elements on all artboards, such as a header or footer. In this document, you'll quickly repeat one artboard's elements on other artboards.

8 Choose the Selection tool, and then in the top-right artboard, select the circular P logo at the bottom center of the artboard.

9 Choose Edit > Cut and then choose Edit > Paste on All Artboards. The logo pastes in the same position on all artboards. It shouldn't be on the first artboard, so simply select that instance of the logo and press Delete.

The multiple artboards in Illustrator are a great example of the way Creative Suite applications specialize in different areas of design. Illustrator artboards are a great way to keep related design pieces together, but they aren't intended to build text-intensive long documents, such as books. If you want to create a long document with automatically numbered pages, a table of contents, and an index, use Adobe InDesign instead.

10 Choose File > Save As, navigate to your Lesson01 folder, name the file ai_artboards_done.ai, and click Save. Then close the document.

Drawing in perspective in Illustrator

When you want to use linear perspective to create depth in Illustrator CS6, it takes no time at all to set up a perspective grid. You can then forget about the technical points of perspective drawing and simply concentrate on your artwork.

1 In Illustrator, choose File > New, click the portrait (tall) Orientation button, and click OK.

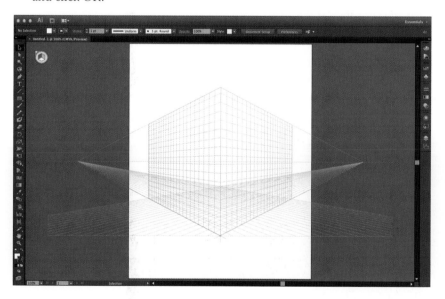

2 Select the Perspective Grid tool (   ). The perspective grid appears.

3 Try dragging the various perspective grid controls:

- The diamond-shaped handles at the bottom-left and bottom-right move the entire grid.

- The diamond-shaped handles at the far-left and far-right sides control the height of the horizon line.

- The circular handles on the left and right sides of the grid change the angles of each plane.

▶ **Tip:** You can save your own presets by choosing View > Perspective Grid > Save Grid as Preset.

4 Choose View > Perspective Grid > One-Point Perspective > -[1P-Normal View] to see a preset for one-point perspective. Then choose View > Perspective Grid > Three-Point Perspective > [3P-Normal View] to see a preset for three-point perspective.

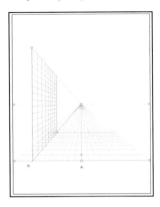 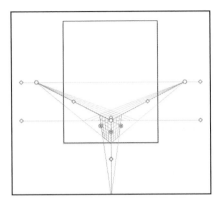

Now that you've seen how the perspective grid works, you can see it in action.

5 Close the current untitled document window without saving changes.

6 In your Lesson01 folder, double-click the file perspective_start.ai. If a Font Problems dialog box appears, click Open. If you don't see the building in the figure below, zoom out to find it and then zoom back in.

This is a building that was drawn using the perspective grid. Now you'll add a couple of windows to it.

7 Choose View > Windows. This brings you to the document view that was saved under the name Windows; if you don't see all six windows in the following figure adjust your document window and magnification as needed. With the Selection tool, select the second window in the top row, and then choose Edit > Copy.

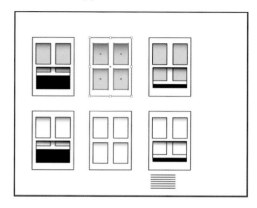

8 Choose View > Initial View.

9 In the plane switching widget, click the empty area outside the cube to make sure no perspective planes are selected, and then choose Edit > Paste.

10 In the Tools panel, select the Perspective Selection tool (▶⊙) which is grouped with the Perspective Grid tool in the Tools panel (to see both, press and hold either tool in the panel). Click the right plane of the cube in the plane switching widget, and then drag the window you pasted into the empty area to the right of the upper window on the right face of the building.

11 Alt/Option-Shift-drag the selected window down to make a copy that lines up with the lower row of windows. As long as you drag with the Perspective Selection tool, the object follows the perspective of the selected plane.

Verifying your document's quality settings

Before saving graphics, it's a good idea to verify the quality of your document.

1 Choose Effect > Document Raster Effects Settings. When the Document Raster Effects Settings dialog box appears, change the default Screen Resolution (72 ppi) to High (300 ppi), and then click OK.

2 Choose File > Save As and save the document into your Lesson01 folder, naming the file **perspective.ai**. In the Illustrator Options dialog box, make sure the options Create PDF Compatible File, Embed ICC Profiles, and Use Compression are all selected, and then click OK.

3 Close the file.

You've completed work on Illustrator elements you'll use in later lessons. Next, you'll get photos ready in Photoshop for projects later in the book.

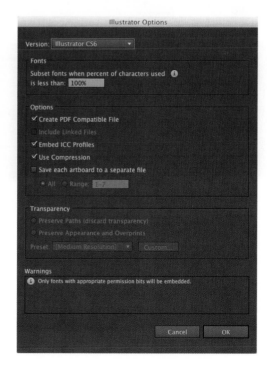

Cropping a Photo in Photoshop

Cropping is a fairly basic task, but one that was completely rethought from the ground up in Adobe Photoshop CS6. Cropping in Photoshop is easier, more intuitive, and less destructive than ever!

1   In your Lesson01 folder in Adobe Bridge, double-click the file Adobe_0367.tif to open it in Photoshop.

2   In Photoshop, select the Crop tool.

The crop rectangle appears around the image, and inside the crop rectangle is a composition overlay that's set to the Rule of Thirds by default.

With the Crop tool selected, the Options bar across the top of the document window presents cropping options, including the current aspect ratio and composition overlay.

3   In the Options bar, click the aspect ratio pop-up menu to examine the preset choices, and then make sure Original Ratio is selected to preserve the current proportions of the image.

If you wanted to specify a custom aspect ratio, you'd enter values in the two blank fields in the Options bar, and the pop-up menu would show Custom Unconstrained selected.

4   Click the Straighten tool in the Options bar, position it over the lamp, and drag it down the stain under the lamp. The image is straightened automatically based on the line you drew.

Although the wall is another strong vertical, because it's off center, we'll leave it as is because it should have a little bit of perspective based on the downward angle of the image.

5   Drag the top-left corner of the crop box down to resize the crop rectangle until the woman appears under one of the Rule of Thirds guides.

6 In the Options bar, click the View pop-up menu to see the list of overlay options, and then choose Cycle Overlay. The overlay changes to the next one in the pop-up menu.

7 Press the **O** key to cycle to the next composition overlay, and continue pressing **O** until you see the composition overlay you like the most.

8 In the Options bar, click the Settings menu (the gear icon) to see options that control how the crop rectangle relates to the area outside the cropped image.

9 In the Settings menu, deselect the Enable Crop Shield option, observe the result, and select it again.

The Crop Shield dims the area outside the image to help you visualize the unapplied crop more effectively, and you can customize it in this menu.

10 Close the Settings menu, and then press Return/Enter to apply the crop with its current settings.

11 Choose File > Save.

Adding Creative Blur in Photoshop

Photoshop contains a wide range of blur filters. Some of them, such as Gaussian Blur, are primarily useful in solving production problems. Photoshop CS6 adds a group of three new blur effects specifically intended for creative purposes: Field Blur, Iris Blur, and Tilt-Shift Blur. Using the popular Tilt-Shift Blur as an example, you'll learn how to control these blur effects using intuitive visual tools. Let's give it a try!

1 With the pink dress image open from the previous exercise, choose Filter > Blur > Tilt-Shift.

Effect controls appear over the image to control the intensity, location, and rate of change for the blur.

2 Drag the center spot to the part of the image you want to remain in sharpest focus—in this case, the model's face.

3 Drag the outer circle to set the amount of blur at the extremes of the effect. As you drag, observe the amount of blur, and also notice that the sliders in the Blur Tools panel move. The outer circle is a direct, visual alternative to dragging the sliders in the panel.

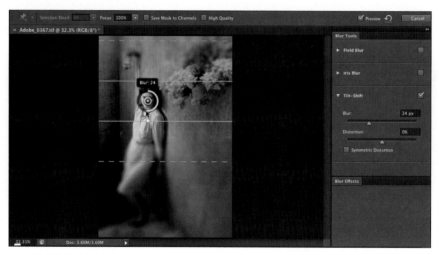

4 Drag the dots on the solid lines to set where you want the blur transition to start and the angle of the blur.

▶ **Tip:** The options in the Blur Effects tab control the quality of light in the areas where you've applied the most blur.

5 Drag the dashed lines to set where the blur transition ends, and where the blur settings are applied at full strength.

6 When you're done, click OK at the top of the document window. (If you don't see the OK button, your workspace may be too narrow; press Return/Enter instead.)

7 Choose File > Save As, navigate to your Lesson01 folder, name the file blur_done.ai, and click Save. Then close the document.

Removing a Background in Photoshop

Extracting a subject from a background is one of the most time-consuming tasks a designer faces. The most difficult part of this task is precisely masking out the edge, especially where hair or fur is involved. The new Truer Edge selection technology in Photoshop CS6 offers better edge detection and masking results in less time.

1   In your Lesson01 folder, double-click the file selection.psd to open it. In the Layers panel, select the Original layer.

2   Choose Select > Load Selection, select model selection from the Channel menu, and then click OK.

3   Choose any selection tool (such as the Rectangular Marquee tool), and then click Refine Edge in the Options bar.

4 Click the View icon and choose On Black from the drop-down menu to make the changes easier to see. Then click the View icon to close the drop-down menu.

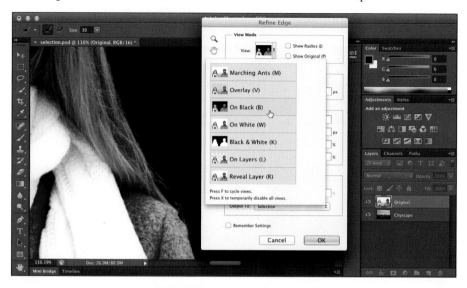

5 Select the Smart Radius check box and set the Radius slider to about 30 px. Watch how the selection edge changes, particularly around the hair. Notice how the selection automatically changes from the jacket to fine hair.

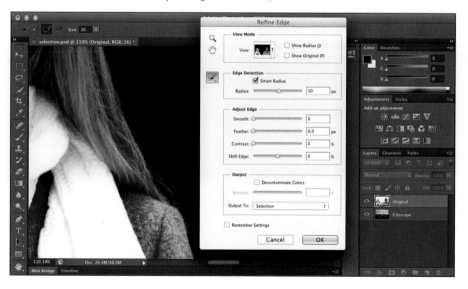

6 In the Refine Edge dialog box, select the Refine Radius tool (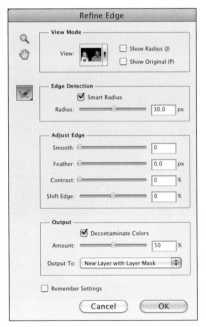). Drag along the hair edge near the woman's shoulder to extend the radius outward to include more of her hair. If you want to reduce the radius, Alt/Option-drag the Refine Radius tool along the outside of the selection.

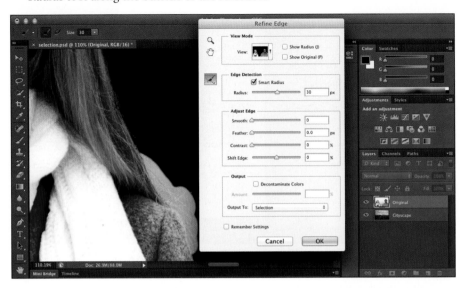

7 Select Decontaminate Colors to remove color fringing by replacing edge colors from the original background with colors from the new background so that the upper layer blends in more effectively. If the initial results don't seem optimal, you can adjust the Amount slider to achieve the most believeable level of color fringe removal.

8 Choose New Layer with Layer Mask from the Output To menu, and then click OK.

9 In the Layers panel, notice the new layer Original Copy and its mask. Make sure to click the eye icon for the Cityscape layer to display it, and notice how the subject is now composited with the cityscape seamlessly, including individual hairs.

10 Choose File > Save As, name the document **selection_done.psd**, and click Save. In the Photoshop Format Options dialog box that appears, click OK without changing the settings. Then close the document.

Removing Unwanted Objects in Photoshop

Another traditionally time-consuming task is filling in areas where unwanted objects have been removed. This normally requires manually cloning and patching the empty area where the object used to be. In Photoshop CS6, Content-Aware Fill automatically matches lighting, tone, texture, and noise to make it look like the deleted area never existed.

1 In your Lesson01 folder, double-click the file content-aware.psd to open it. With the Lasso tool, make a rough selection around the man.

2 Press the Delete key. In the Fill dialog box, make sure Content-Aware is selected in the Use menu, and click OK.

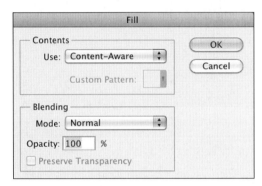

3 The man is deleted and filled in with the surrounding wall texture. Choose Select > Deselect to view the image without the selection.

4 Close the document, and if you're asked if you want to save changes, click Save

Another valuable use for Content-Aware Fill is removing wires, graffiti, or other fine or thin objects. For this task, it's better to use the Spot Healing Brush in Content-Aware mode.

5 In your Lesson01 folder, double-click the file content-aware_spot.psd to open it. Select the Spot Healing Brush, and in the Options bar, make sure the Content-Aware option is selected.

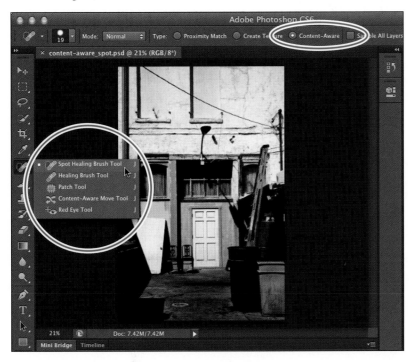

6 Drag the Spot Healing Brush along the wire at the top of the image. When you release the mouse, observe how the wire has been removed seamlessly because the surrounding textures and window frames have been detected and matched.

 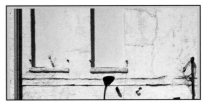

7 Try removing other fixtures in the image as well. When you're done, close the document, and if you're asked if you want to save changes, click Save.

Moving Objects Seamlessly in Photoshop

In photographic images, it can be a challenge to reposition objects within the image because cutting out an object in one part of an image leaves behind a blank hole. In Photoshop CS6, the Content-Aware Move tool seamlessly fills in the former position of an object while also blending the object into its new position, saving a lot of time.

1　In your Lesson01 folder in Adobe Bridge, double-click the file Move.jpg.

2　Select the Lasso tool, and draw a selection marquee around the girl on the right. It can be a rough selection; don't take the time to be exact.

3　Press and hold the mouse on the Spot Healing Brush tool to reveal the tool menu, and then choose the Content-Aware Move tool.

4   Using the Content-Aware Move tool, drag the selected girl to a different part of the image, and then choose Select > Deselect. Notice how the area formerly occupied by the girl has been filled in, and the girl is blended in with her new surroundings.

5   Choose File > Save As, and choose Photoshop from the Format menu. Navigate to your Lesson01 folder, , name the file move_done.psd, and click Save. Then close the document.

Naturally, this works best if the old and new backgrounds are similar. There may be times when you'll have to touch up the edges a bit, but in most cases you'll have saved so much time that it'll be more than worth it.

Wrapping Up

You've learned many of the Adobe Creative Suite 6 Design & Web Premium features that are important for preparing assets for projects. Throughout this book, you'll see how the assets you worked on in this lesson fit into larger workflows.

Review questions

1   How can you speed up the process of finding files and folders in Adobe Bridge?

2   Why would you use Adobe Bridge to synchronize your color settings when working within Adobe Creative Suite 6 applications?

3   What is so special about the Blob Brush tool in Adobe Illustrator CS6?

4   What are some practical uses for artboards?

5   How is Content-Aware Fill useful in Adobe Photoshop CS6?

Review answers

1   Select a file or folder and choose File > Add to Favorites. The file or folder will appear in the Favorites panel in the left panel group of the Adobe Bridge window where you have easy access to it. Alternatively, you can drag the file or folder—or even an application—directly into the Favorites panel.

2   Adobe Bridge provides centralized access to your project files and enables you to synchronize color settings across all color-managed Creative Suite 6 applications. This synchronization ensures that colors look the same in all Adobe Creative Suite 6 components. If color settings are not synchronized, a warning message appears at the top of the Color Settings dialog box in each application. It is highly recommended that you synchronize color settings before starting to work with new or existing documents.

3   While sketching with the Blob Brush tool, you can create a filled vector shape with a single outline, even when your strokes overlap. All the separate paths merge into a single object, which can easily be edited. Using the Blob Brush tool in combination with the Eraser tool enables you to make your shapes perfect, keeping a single, smooth outline.

4   You can use artboards to organize related components of a project in a single Illustrator file, such as an envelope, business card, and letterhead; maintain multiple pages of an interactive online project; or store multiple versions of a project.

5   Content-Aware Fill saves time because it automatically fills in deleted objects by matching the lighting, tone, texture, and noise of surrounding areas instead of requiring you to manually patch the area.

2 CREATING A PRINT LAYOUT

Lesson Overview

In this lesson you'll learn the skills and techniques you need to put together a sophisticated print magazine:

- Using Mini Bridge and Adobe Bridge to preview and select files

- Creating a document in InDesign

- Working with layer comps in Photoshop files

- Adjusting raw images

- Importing and styling text

- Laying out graphics efficiently

- Working with transparency

 You'll probably need between one and two hours to complete this lesson.

Quickly identify and import files using Adobe Bridge and Mini Bridge. Add text and graphics in a variety of file formats and take advantage of advanced layout tools. Then prepare your documents for high-quality printed output.

● **Note:** Before you
start working on this
lesson, make sure
that you've installed
the Creative Suite
6 software on your
computer and that you
have correctly copied
the Lessons folder
from the DVD in the
back of this book onto
your computer's hard
drive (see "Copying the
Classroom in a Book
files" on page 3).

Inspecting and Selecting Documents with Adobe Bridge

If you've ever looked at a folder full of files and were unsure about which one you should open, take advantage of Adobe Bridge. Using Adobe Bridge to find the right document is often easier than using the standard Open dialog box, because Adobe Bridge gives you tools to inspect documents without opening them. Adobe Bridge can preview many file types produced in Design Premium. For InDesign files, Adobe Bridge can display the fonts and links in an InDesign document, and you can preview the document's pages.

You'll use Adobe Bridge to locate a partially completed InDesign document that you will use for the exercises in this lesson. The document represents the latest issue of a printed magazine.

1   Start Adobe Bridge, and make sure the Essentials workspace is selected at the top of the Adobe Bridge window.

2   Navigate to the Lesson02 folder on your hard drive. Within that folder, select, but don't open, the file Magazine_Start.indt.

3   In the Preview panel, click the arrow buttons under the document preview to see the other page in the InDesign document. Using Adobe Bridge to page through InDesign documents without opening them can save you a lot of time.

4   Notice the chain-link badge at the top-right corner of the selected InDesign document icon in the Content panel. This badge indicates that you can inspect the links in the InDesign document. You'll do that next.

5   Scroll the Metadata panel until you find the Linked Files pane, where you can view a list of the files linked to this InDesign document. Click the disclosure triangle to reveal the list.

    Above the Linked Files pane is the Fonts pane, where you can see which fonts are used in the InDesign document.

6   Select the file Magazine_Start.indt, and then choose File > Open With > Adobe InDesign CS6 (default).

    Magazine_Start.indt is a template—it opens as a new, untitled document (see the sidebar "Jump-starting design and production using templates"). You'll save this document under a new name; the template file will remain unchanged so that you can always go back to it if you need to start over.

7   In InDesign, choose File > Save. In the Save As dialog box, navigate to the Lesson02 folder, name the document **Magazine.indd**, choose InDesign CS6 document from the Save As Type/Format menu, and then click Save.

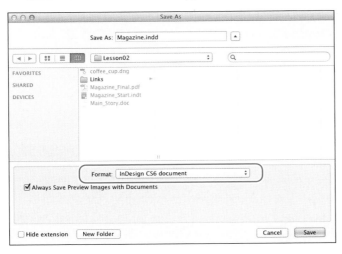

Modifying an InDesign Document

Now that you have created a document from the InDesign template, you can adjust it just as you can any other InDesign document. You can replace illustrations and photos, add and stylize text, and even change the document layout settings you've acquired from the template.

Navigating through the document

Before making any changes to the document, navigate through its pages so you can plan which elements you'd like to customize.

Tip: The visibility of menu items can be customized in InDesign. Selecting a predefined workspace may result in some menu items being hidden. If you can't find the menu item you're looking for, choose Show All Menu Items at the bottom of the menu, when available.

Tip: If graphics on the layout display at a low resolution, you can display them with greater detail (as in the figure for step 2) by choosing View > Display Performance > High Quality Display. Note that High Quality Display takes longer to redraw.

1 Choose Window > Workspace > [Advanced] to lay out all the panels you'll need for this lesson and make all menu commands visible.

2 Use the navigation buttons in the lower-left corner of your document window to navigate through the pages of the magazine. Then use the menu next to the current page number to return to the first page.

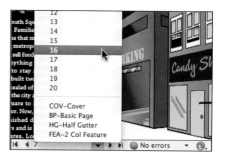

3 Click the Pages button in the right panel bin to open the Pages panel. If necessary, enlarge the Pages panel by dragging its lower-right corner downward so you can see preview images of all pages. Double-clicking a page in the Pages panel will open that page in the main document window. Double-clicking the page number under the preview image will center the page spread in the main document window.

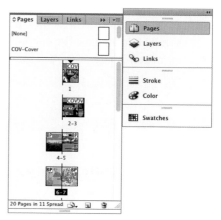

4 Click the Pages button in the right panel bin again to close the Pages panel.

Jump-starting design and production using templates

When you produce a certain type of document repeatedly, such as a monthly issue of a magazine, you can save time by starting each issue from a template. A template is an InDesign document that contains any custom design elements and production settings you save into it, such as master page layouts, background elements, placeholder frames for text and graphics, and text and object styles. When you open a template, it opens as a new, untitled InDesign document. Using templates as the basis for frequently created documents is faster and easier than opening an old version and deleting all the content.

To create your own template from any InDesign document, choose File > Save As, and then choose InDesign CS6 Template from the Format menu. Template documents use the .indt filename extension.

Viewing the reference document

In the Lesson02 folder is a PDF version of the completed magazine that you can use as a reference as you work through this lesson. This time we'll use Mini Bridge, a version of Adobe Bridge that you can use as a panel inside InDesign for easier access to the assets you want to bring into an InDesign document.

1   In InDesign, choose Window > Mini Bridge. If you see a Launch Bridge button, click it now.

2   Navigate to the Lesson02 folder, and select the file Magazine_Final.pdf.

3   Right-click/Control-click Magazine_Final.pdf, and choose Open.

4   In Acrobat choose View > Page Display > Two Page View and View > Zoom > Fit Width. Then use the arrow keys on your keyboard to navigate through the spreads.

5   When you're done, return to InDesign. You can leave the PDF document open for reference.

6   Close the Mini Bridge panel.

Working with multiple page sizes

The magazine cover looks good, but to give it a little more interest, the client wants to extend the right side of the cover using a foldover flap. You'll create this by adding a page to the cover to create a spread. In addition, the page you add to the spread will use a smaller, narrower page size.

1　In the Pages panel, double-click page 1, right-click/Control-click the Page 1 thumbnail, choose Insert Pages, and in the dialog box that appears, click OK.

Because you created the new page from Page 1, it's part of the Page 1 spread.

2　In the Tools panel, click the Page tool (⬚) , and then click the new page you created. As you do this, the Control panel displays options for the selected page.

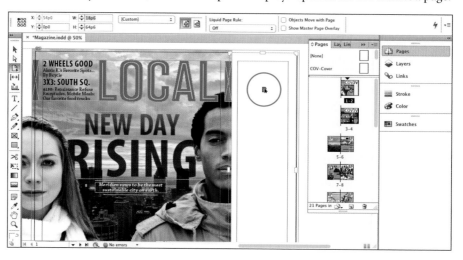

▶ **Tip:** To adjust the bleed and slug areas, choose File > Document Setup. If you don't see the Bleed and Slug options, click the More Options button.

3　In the Control panel, change the page width (W) to **18p6**.

4　In the Layers panel, click the disclosure triangles to the left of the Text layer and Background Art layer to reveal sublayers and the objects on those layers.

5 Click the square icon to the right of the <Cover_Models.psd> object label to select it.

6 In the Tools panel, click the Selection tool (➤). Drag the handle in the middle of the right edge to extend the graphic across the new page until the graphic is 93p1.6 wide, all the way to the right edge of the bleed area. The Control panel and the tool tip display the width as you drag.

7 Choose Edit > Deselect All.

You could have also selected the graphic by clicking it with the Selection tool, but on a busy layout like this one, using the Layers panel can be a more direct way of ensuring that you select exactly the object you want.

Selecting and editing frames that are stacked behind other frames

The sunrise image should also be extended across the new page, but you can't select it by clicking because it's completely behind the Cover_Models.psd image. Fortunately, there's more than one way to select it.

> ▶ **Tip:** You can restack objects by dragging them up and down in the Layers panel.

1 With the Selection tool, hold down the Ctrl/Command key, and then click the sunrise image. The first time you click, the bounding box for the Cover_Models.psd image may activate. Keep the Ctrl/Command key pressed and click again until the blue outline of the sunrise image activates. You can confirm this by noting which object in the Layers panel has a selected square to the right of it.

2   Once the sunrise image's frame is selected, you can drag the handle in the middle of the right edge until it is 74 picas wide. Of course, this works only when the image is larger than the frame that crops it in InDesign.

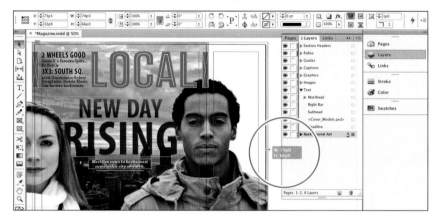

3   Save your changes.

The second way to select the sunrise image would be to locate it in the Layers panel and click the square to the right of it, as you did with the Cover_Models.psd image.

Placing a Photoshop file with layer comps

Navigate to the last page, the back cover. Currently, the back cover is blank. You will first place the back page photo into the frame provided for it, and then make adjustments to the image in Photoshop.

1   Use the Selection tool to select the frame on the last page.

Note: If your placed graphic does not look as smooth as shown in the illustration on this page, choose View > Display Performance > High Quality Display.

2   Choose File > Place. Navigate to the Links folder inside the Lesson02 folder. Select the file wifi_laptop.psd, select both Show Import Options and Replace Selected Items, and then click Open.

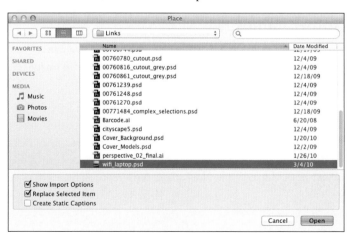

3 In the Image Import Options (wifi_laptop.psd) dialog box, and make sure the Show Preview option is selected. In the Layers tab, notice that all of the layers are turned on. Choose Sponsor On from the Layer Comp menu; the preview thumbnail updates to show the Local logo in the bottom-right corner. Click OK.

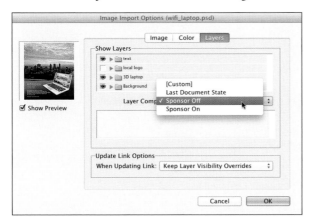

Because you enabled Replace Selected Item in the Place dialog box, the imported Photoshop file fills the frame you selected instead of being placed independently on the layout.

4 To view the cover without page frames and guide lines, click and hold the Screen Mode button at the bottom of the Tools panel and choose Preview. When you're done previewing, choose Normal from the same menu. You can also toggle between Normal and Preview by pressing the W key.

▶ **Tip:** You can hide or show each layer independently. Layer comps are just a convenient way to hide or show preselected groups of layers.

The sunset would look better if it was a little more intense, so you will now use Photoshop to alter the color balance of the sky.

▶ **Tip:** You can also do step 5 by choosing Edit > Edit Original, or by Alt/Option-clicking the image.

5   Use the Selection tool to select the frame containing the image and choose
    Edit > Edit With > Adobe Photoshop CS6 (default).

6   In the Layers panel in Photoshop, click the disclosure triangle next to the
    Background layer group to reveal its contents. Select the Background Image
    layer at the bottom of the Layers panel.

7   In the Adjustments panel, click the Color Balance icon to add a new Color
    Balance adjustment layer immediately above the selected layer.

8   In the Color Balance panel, make sure Midtones is selected, and then enter **25**
    for the Cyan/Red slider, **0** for the Magenta/Green slider, and **-12** for the Red/
    Blue slider. Leave Preserve Luminosity selected.

Because the document now contains a layer that wasn't included in the original layer
comps, you'll learn how to update the layer comps so they're properly preserved
when you return to InDesign.

9 Open the Layer Comps panel (Window > Layer Comps). Two layer comps have already been defined, named Sponsor Off and Sponsor On. Click the box to the left of the Sponsor On layer name to enable that layer comp, and notice the effect it has on the visibility of the layers in the Layers panel and in the image.

A layer comp is simply a snapshot of the visibility, position, and layer style settings for various layers in the Layers panel. You may notice that the Color Balance layer you created was turned off when you turned on the Sponsor On layer comp. The reason is that that layer didn't exist when the layer comp was originally saved.

10 Turn on the Color Balance layer, make sure Sponsor On is highlighted in the Layer Comps panel (but don't turn it on), and then choose Update Layer Comp from the Layer Comps panel menu. Now the Sponsor On layer comp includes the Color Balance adjustment layer. You can repeat this process for the Sponsor Off layer comp: Turn on the layer comp, turn on the Color Balance adjustment layer, and update the layer comp.

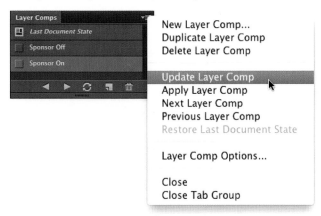

When placing a Photoshop file containing layer comps in InDesign, you can choose which version—or layer comp—you want to use in your publication without having to reopen and adjust the file in Photoshop.

11 Save changes, close the document, and then switch back to InDesign. An alert may appear, letting you know that the graphic has changed; click OK.

12 With the back cover image still selected in InDesign, choose Object > Object Layer Options. From the Layer Comp menu in the Object Layer Options dialog box, choose Sponsor On, select the Preview check box to see the effect, and then click OK.

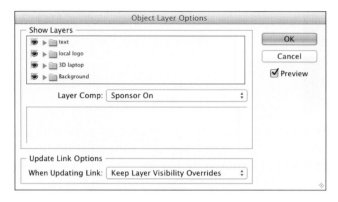

13 Choose File > Save.

Working with camera raw images

● **Note:** Camera raw is not a single format. Each camera sensor model may have a different raw format and filename extension. Most camera raw formats can be converted to the DNG (Adobe Digital Negative) format.

Camera raw format files are now common for high-quality digital photographs. The Camera Raw plug-in for Adobe Photoshop enables you to adjust a raw image and to then save it in a file format that can be placed in InDesign.

1 In InDesign navigate to page 17. If not already selected, choose View > Screen Mode > Normal. If you don't see guidelines on the page, choose View > Grids & Guides > Show Guides.

2 Select the empty graphics frame on page 17 and choose Object > Fitting > Frame Fitting Options. Select Auto-Fit, choose Fill Frame Proportionally, and click the center of the Align From proxy. These options ensure that no matter the size of the image, it will be sized to fit the frame and centered within it, saving you time in fitting the image to the frame.

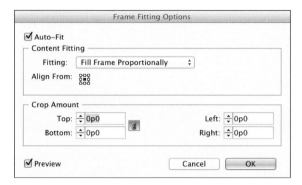

3 Click OK.

4 Switch to Adobe Bridge, and in the Lesson02 folder double-click the raw image file named coffee_cup.dng. The image will open in Photoshop in the Camera Raw dialog box.

● **Note:** The reason you need to switch to Adobe Bridge is that Mini Bridge displays only the file formats its host program can import directly, and InDesign can't import DNG files.

5 To adjust the white balance in a camera raw image, you can choose from a predefined setting or pick a reference area within the image. Explore the different settings in the White Balance menu in the Basic panel and note the effect on the image colors. To adjust the color relative to an area in the image that should be a neutral mid-gray, select the White Balance tool (🖋) from the Tools panel and then click inside the reference area. Clicking the White Balance tool on the coffee cup neutralizes the image colors. However, this photo is intended to convey a warm coffee-shop atmosphere, so restore the original white balance by choosing As Shot from the White Balance menu.

6   The image is a little flat, so it could use more contrast. To have Camera Raw determine a starting point for correction, click the underlined Auto text. From this point you can refine the automatic correction by dragging the sliders. The image is a little dark now, so increase the Exposure value to about 0.15.

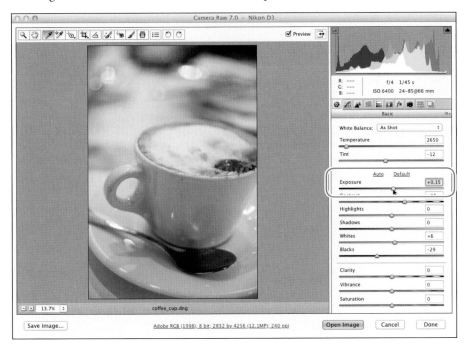

7   To specify a fixed aspect ratio for the Crop tool, click and hold the Crop tool button in the toolbar, and then select an aspect ratio from the menu. We chose 4 to 5 to approximate the proportions of the frame in the InDesign layout, with a little room to spare.

8 Using the Crop tool, drag across the image to create a crop rectangle, as shown in the illustration.

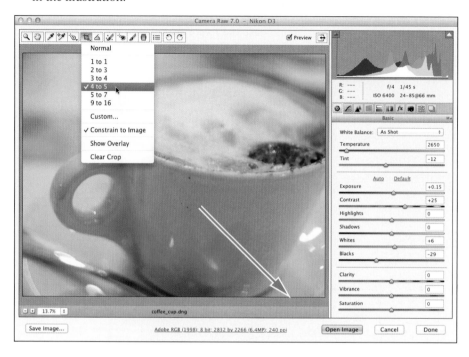

At this point you could click Open Image to open the image in Photoshop and make further adjustments if necessary. For this exercise, you'll just save the file in a format that can be used in InDesign.

9 Click the Save Image button in the lower-left corner of the Camera Raw dialog box. In the Save Options dialog box, choose Save in New Location from the Destination menu, and select the Links folder inside the Lesson02 folder as the destination for the saved file. Type **_cropped** to add it to the document name, select Photoshop for the file format, and then click Save.

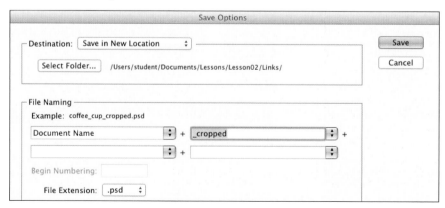

10 Click Done to close the Camera Raw dialog box and return to InDesign.

11 In InDesign use Mini Bridge to navigate to the Links folder inside the Lesson02 folder.

12 Click the Sort icon, choose By Date Modified, and deselect Ascending Order. This brings the coffee cup image to the top of the list because it's the most recent file you modified.

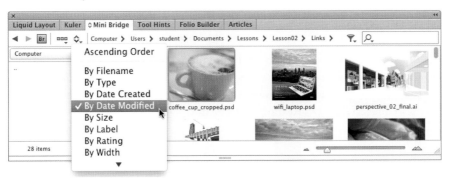

13 Drag the file coffee_cup_cropped.psd and drop it into the empty frame on page 17. The coffee cup image is automatically sized within and centered in the frame because of the Auto Fit settings you applied in step 2.

14 Move the mouse over the coffee cup image you just placed. Notice the Content Grabber in the middle of the image. Drag this indicator to move the image within the frame. The Content Grabber lets you adjust the position of the image within the frame without having to select a separate tool.

15 Save your changes.

Importing and styling text

You can enter text directly into an InDesign document by typing into the text frames. For longer text passages, however, it is more common to import text from an external text document. You can style the text as part of the import process or manually change the text appearance later.

1 In InDesign navigate to page 12 of the magazine document.

The text columns of the feature story are filled with placeholder text. You'll replace the placeholder text with text from a Word document.

2 Select the Type tool in the Tools panel and place the cursor anywhere in the text in the two main text columns on page 12. Choose Edit > Select All. The text in both columns is selected because the text columns are linked. These text frames are also linked with the text frames on the next few pages.

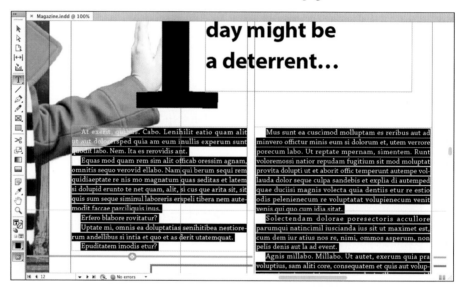

3 Choose File > Place. In the Place dialog box navigate to the Lesson02 folder, select the file Main_Story.doc, select both Show Import Options and Replace Selected Item, and click Open.

4 Under Formatting in the Microsoft Word Import Options (Main_Story.doc) dialog box, select Preserve Styles And Formatting From Text And Tables and Customize Style Import. Click the Style Mapping button.

The Style Mapping dialog box enables you to match type styles defined in the Word document to type styles defined in the InDesign document. If you set up the styles with identical names, InDesign can perform the mapping automatically.

In this case, the Style Mapping dialog box shows that the Microsoft Word style Sidebar Bullet List doesn't match up with any style names in InDesign, so you'll have to map this style manually.

5 In the InDesign Style column in the Style Mapping dialog box, click [New Paragraph Style] to the right of the Microsoft Word style Sidebar Bullet List, and choose Sidebar Bulleted List. This maps the Word style to the InDesign style, which in this case is correct because the two styles are actually the same but were named slightly differently in the two programs.

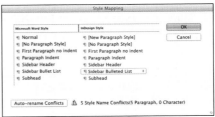

6 Click OK to close the Style Mapping dialog box, and then click OK to close the Import Options dialog box.

The imported text replaces the text in the two text frames and in the threaded text frames in the pages that follow, and the styles in the text take on the formatting defined by the same style names in InDesign. The text on page 12 overlaps the woman's arm; you'll fix that a little later.

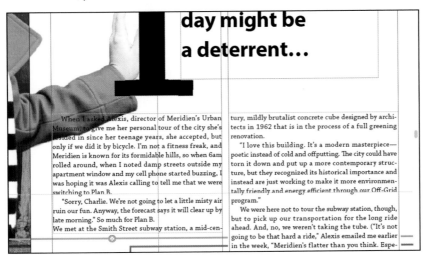

7 Navigate to page 13 to see how the story continues through the threaded frames to the next spread.

Applying paragraph styles

In the story you just imported, one of the headings has the wrong style applied. It's body text, but it should be a heading. You'll fix this by applying the correct paragraph style.

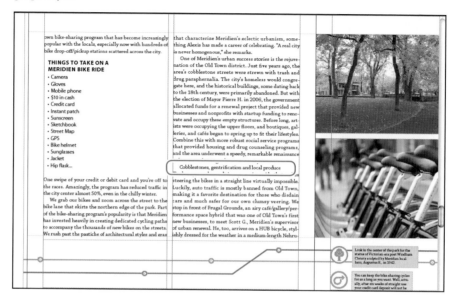

1 While viewing page 13, open the Paragraph Styles panel (Window > Styles > Paragraph Styles).

2 Select the Text tool from the Tools panel, and click to place the flashing cursor inside the heading "Cobblestones, gentrification and local produce" almost two-thirds of the way down the second column. For a paragraph style, it is not necessary to select the entire paragraph.

3 In the Paragraph Styles panel, select the Subhead paragraph style. Notice the change in the text in the document window.

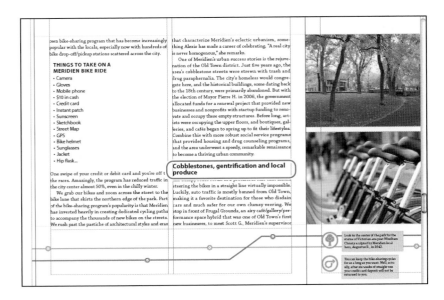

4 Save your changes.

Wrapping text around frames

Now that the text is formatted properly, it's time to take care of the text overlapping the woman's arm on page 12.

1 With the Selection tool, click the woman's arm.

Although not currently visible, this image contains a clipping path that was drawn in Adobe Photoshop to cut the image out of its red background. You can also use this path as a text wrap boundary.

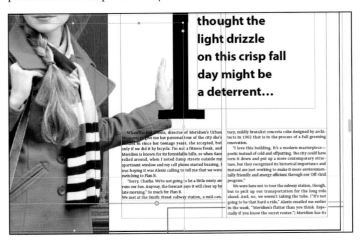

2   In the Text Wrap panel (Window > Text Wrap), click the third button from the left in the top row. This button wraps text around the shape of the object's frame.

3   In the Text Wrap panel, choose Photoshop Path from the Contour Options: Type menu. There is only one clipping path stored in the document, Path 1, which appears in the Path menu. The clipping path is now used as the frame for the image, hiding all parts of the image that lie outside the frame path.

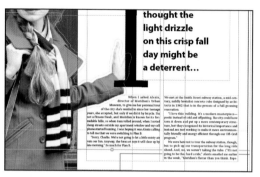

Note that a 9-point wrap offset distance is specified in the Text Wrap panel. You can adjust this number to control the distance of the text wrap from the object frame, but you don't need to make an adjustment here.

If you wanted to edit the shape of the object frame, you could select the Direct Selection tool to move the points on the frame.

Splitting paragraphs within columns and spanning paragraphs across columns

There's some additional layout work to be done on page 13. To improve the composition of the page, you'll change the two columns on the page to three columns, and you'll convert some of the text into a sidebar. Fortunately, this will be as simple as selecting text and choosing options in the Control panel.

1   Go to page 13, and with the Selection tool, click the two-column text frame.

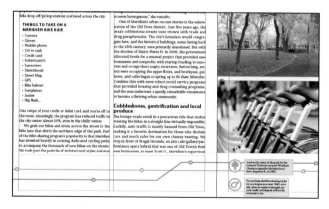

2   Choose Object > Text Frame Options, change the Number of columns to **3**, and
click OK.

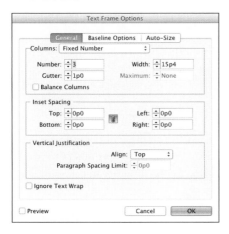

3   With the Type tool, select the bullet list in the first column. (Don't select the
heading.)

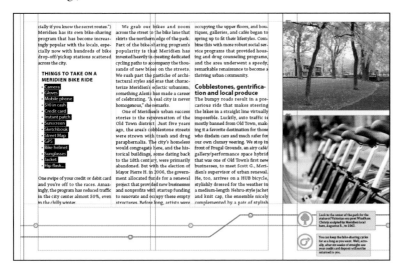

4   Make sure the Control panel is in Paragraph Formatting mode (the paragraph
symbol is selected at the left edge), and choose Split 2 from the Span Columns
menu in the Control panel.

5 Click the Type tool in the "Cobblestones, gentrification…" heading and choose Span 3 from the same Span Columns menu in the Control panel.

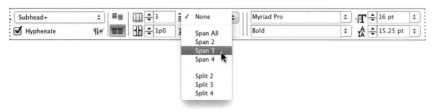

6 In the Layers panel, if necessary click the disclosure triangle next to the Text layer to expand it. Then click in the eye column for the Blue Box object to make it visible behind the sidebar. The box was added by the designer to accommodate the sidebar.

 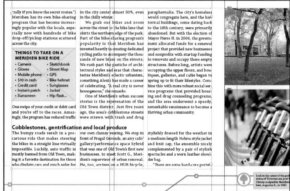

Laying out multiple photos in a grid

You can quickly and easily lay out many photos at once for publications such as catalogs and yearbooks. InDesign simplifies and accelerates this process by letting you place multiple photos into a grid you create as you import the images and by using metadata inside images to generate automatic image captions on the layout.

▶ **Tip:** The four files are easiest to select together if the sort icon in Mini Bridge is set to sort by filename, because the numbers in the filenames are sequential.

1 Go to page 15, and in the Layers panel, select the layer Graphics. This ensures that images you import into InDesign will be placed on the Graphics layer.

2 In Mini Bridge, navigate to the Links folder. Select the four files 01_Fruitstand.psd, 02_Berries.psd, 03_Corn.psd, and 04_Flowers.psd, and drag all four selected items to page 15 of the InDesign layout.

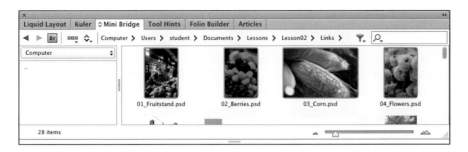

3 Position the loaded Place cursor at the intersection of the left margin and the cyan guide below the text frame on page 15. Begin dragging, and while the mouse button is still down, press the right arrow key once and then the up arrow once to create a 2 x 2 grid. Continue dragging to the bottom-right corner of the page to the intersection of the lower ruler guide and the right margin guide, and then release the mouse. Leave the images selected.

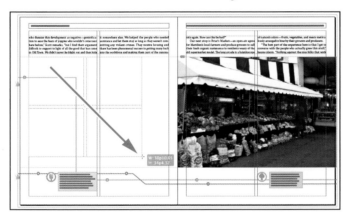

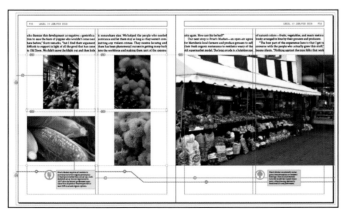

The images are set to fit within their frames, but you want these images to fill their frames while maintaining their proportions.

4   Choose Object > Fitting > Frame Fitting Options. In the dialog box, select Fill Frame Proportionally in the Fitting menu, check the Auto-Fit option, then select the center point in the Align From proxy. Click OK.

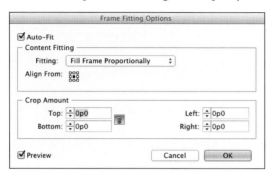

Creating live captions

Keywords, captions, and other metadata are becoming increasingly critical to print and online publishing. One way you can use metadata to enhance your publishing workflow is to automatically generate captions next to photos on the layout.

1   Choose Object > Captions > Caption Setup.

2   In the Caption Setup dialog box, set the first Metadata menu to Description. The other items in the menu are all forms of metadata that can potentially be included in an image by entering it using an application such as Adobe Bridge or as shot data added by a camera.

3   If you see a second Metadata Caption line, click the minus sign after the end of the line to remove it.

4   In the Position and Style section, set the Offset to **1p0** (one pica, zero points), choose Captions from the Paragraph Style menu, and then choose Captions from the Layer menu. Click OK.

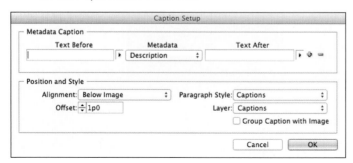

5　Use the Selection tool to select the image of the market on page 16. Zoom in to the bottom-left corner of the market image.

6　Choose Object > Captions > Generate Live Caption, and watch a caption appear to the specifications you set up in the Caption Setup dialog box.

● **Note:** If the caption displays an error, such as <No intersecting link>, make sure the caption text frame touches the graphics text frame.

This is a live caption because if the image description is changed (for example, using the Metadata panel in Adobe Bridge or Photoshop) when the image is updated in InDesign, the caption will update automatically. A live caption aligns with the left edge of the selected image by default; in this case that puts the caption in the gutter. You'll now move the caption's left edge so that it will be readable in the bound magazine.

7　With the caption's text frame selected, drag the bottom-left handle of the text frame horizontally so that it snaps to the page margin.

Shortcuts for editing objects

Repetitive layout tasks, such as aligning and distributing objects or customizing frame corners, are easy and quick in InDesign CS6. You saw an example of this earlier when you used the Content Grabber to recompose an image inside a frame. You can take advantage of other layout tricks in InDesign CS6.

1　Select the coffee cup image on page 17, and drag a corner of its frame to make the frame smaller. Notice that the image inside the frame resizes as well.

2　With the image still selected, deselect the Auto Fit check box in the Control panel, and drag the corner of the image frame to enlarge it. This time the image doesn't scale with the frame. Choose Edit > Undo Resize Item, select Auto Fit, and drag the corner to enlarge the frame back to its original size. Then deselect the image.

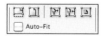 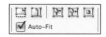

You control how Auto Fit works in the same Frame Fitting Options dialog box you worked with earlier.

3　On page 15, hold down the Shift key as you click to select all of the four images you placed into a grid. Make sure Auto Fit is selected in the Control panel.

4　In the Layers panel, click in the eye column to hide the Background Art layer.

5   Select the Gap tool in the Tools panel, and then position it in the gap between any two of the four images. You may want to zoom in so that the gaps are larger.

6   Drag the Gap tool to control the space between the frames.

7   Shift-drag the Gap tool to adjust only the gap nearest the cursor. Each modifier key changes how the Gap tool works, so experiment with holding down the Alt/Option and Ctrl/Command keys as you drag the Gap tool.

Now you'll use the Gap tool temporarily, using a feature called spring-loaded cursors. It's a quick way to use different tools with fewer trips to the Tools panel. Spring-loaded cursors take advantage of another time-saver: shortcut keys for tools. U is the shortcut key for the Gap tool.

8   Click the Selection tool in the Tools panel. This is the tool you'll probably be using most of the time.

▶ **Tip:** When releasing a spring-loaded tool you're dragging, release the mouse button first and then the tool key.

9   Position the Selection tool over a gap between images, and then press and hold the U key. Notice that the cursor changes to the Gap tool; continue to hold down the U key as you drag to adjust the gap between the images. Release the mouse and then the U key; the cursor returns to the Selection tool.

Normally, pressing a shortcut key permanently switches tools. Spring-loading the cursor lets the new tool snap back to the old tool as soon as you release a shortcut key. Think of the difference this way: To use a shortcut key, briefly tap it; to use a shortcut key as a spring-loaded shortcut, hold it down until you're done.

10 With the Selection tool, click the image of berries, and then click the yellow control near the top-right corner of the image. The frame handles at the corners turn into diamond handles. These diamond handles let you customize the shapes of the frame corners.

▶ **Tip:** To learn the shortcut keys, hold the cursor over various tools in the Tools panel until their tool tips appear; shortcut keys are listed in the tool tips.

● **Note:** If you don't see the yellow handles, choose View > Extras > Show Live Corners. Also, make sure View > Screen Mode is set to Normal.

11 Drag any of the yellow diamond handles to adjust the corner radius of all corners. The corner radius value appears in the Corner Options section of the Control panel; choose a corner shape from the Corner Shape menu below the radius value. Shift-drag a diamond handle to adjust just one corner, or Alt/Option-click a diamond handle to change the corner shape.

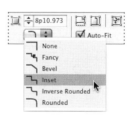

▶ **Tip:** Alt/Option-click the Corner Options icon in the Control panel to open the Corner Options dialog box.

12 In the Layers panel, click in the eye column for the Background Art layer to make that layer visible again.

Tracking text changes

Get to final copy faster by tracking text changes directly in your InDesign document. You can write, edit, and mark up text in InDesign CS6 without needing to import separate text files and remap styles every time there are copy changes.

▶ **Tip:** Another way to change corner shapes is to Alt/Option-drag a corner handle.

1   Navigate to page 13. Choose Window > Editorial > Assignments, and then choose User from the Assignments panel menu. Enter a User Name, choose a Color, and click OK.

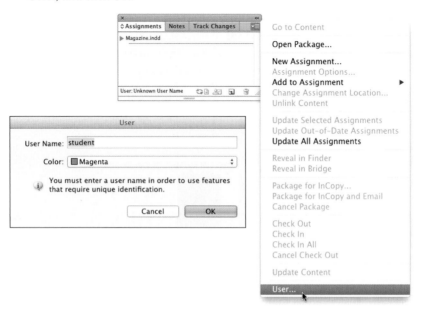

2   With the Type tool, click to place an insertion point inside the text story. Choose Window > Editorial > Track Changes. The top-left button in the Track Changes panel controls whether change tracking is enabled, and the next button controls whether changes are visible. Make sure both buttons are on.

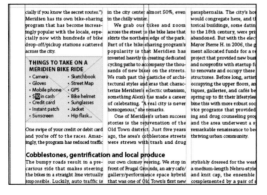

3   In the "Things to Take on a Meridien Bike Ride" sidebar, select the text 10 and type 25.

4 Choose Edit > Edit in Story Editor to open the Story Editor window and note the highlight color. Click in the highlighted text and notice that the Track Changes panel indicates that you are the user who edited the text.

If you see text highlighted in other colors, that's text edited by other users whom you can identify in the Track Changes panel.

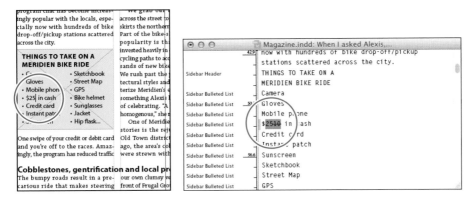

5 Click inside the highlighted text you edited, and click the Accept Change button in the Track Changes panel.

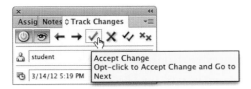

6 When you're done, close the Story Editor window and the Track Changes panel.

Preparing for Printing

You've completed the design of the magazine. Because the document contains transparency effects, there are a few more adjustments necessary to get the best print results.

Transparent areas in a document need to be flattened—or rasterized—when printed. For best results, flattening should be done as the last possible step in your print workflow—normally, it is performed by your print service provider. To keep transparency effects live until they need to be flattened, preserve the layers by saving your InDesign documents (or placed Illustrator or Photoshop files) in a native format.

You can help minimize the effects of flattening if you send your document output to devices that support the latest versions of PDF. To preserve transparency effects rather than flattening them when exporting a document as a PDF intended for printing, save your file in a format compatible with Adobe PDF 1.5 (Acrobat 5.0) or later by selecting the PDF/X-4 PDF export preset, for example. The Adobe PDF Print Engine (APPE)—widely embraced by OEM partners and print service providers since first released in 2006 and updated to version 2 in 2008—uses native rasterizing for PDF documents, ensuring file integrity from start to finish in a PDF-based design workflow. To learn more about the APPE, go to www.adobe.com/products/pdfprintengine.

In InDesign the Flattener Preview panel helps you identify which areas will be most affected by the flattening process. You'll look at how that works next.

Previewing how transparency will affect output

1   In InDesign navigate to page 8 of the magazine document.

● **Note:** If the background art looks chunky, choose View > Display Performance > High Quality Display. The Display Performance setting has no effect on how transparency is rendered when exported or printed.

2   To see which areas of your document are affected by transparency effects, open the Flattener Preview panel (Window > Output > Flattener Preview), select Transparent Objects from the Highlight menu, and choose [High Resolution] from the Preset menu. Then in the Highlight menu, select these commands in turn: All Affected Objects, Affected Graphics, and All Rasterized Regions. When you're done, choose Transparent Objects.

The areas affected by each Highlight option are highlighted in red, such as the text frame in the lower-right corner of the page. You can use the Effects panel to find out why that object is highlighted. Specifically, you're looking for a blend mode other than Normal in the menu at the top of the Effects panel, an Opacity lower than 100%, or an applied effect.

3   Using the Selection tool, click the text frame.

4   If the Effects panel is not visible, choose Window > Effects.

5   Double-click the group to select the frame inside the group. Now that the text frame is selected, the Effects panel reveals that the Fill uses the Multiply blend mode and is set to 85% Opacity. These are the options that create transparency in this object.

If the Flattener Preview panel reveals potential issues with how transparency will affect part of your document during output, you can decide what to do about those issues. For example, if you see that type or highly detailed vector graphics will become rasterized, you might decide to change the design to avoid the problem by moving critical objects so that they don't overlap objects that use transparency or by avoiding the use of transparency in that area.

One thing to watch out for is text placed behind objects with transparency effects. Transparency affects all objects placed lower—or farther back—in the display stacking order. Printed text might not look as crisp as it should if it was converted to outlines and rasterized behind an object with a transparency effect, so when possible, it's best to keep text in front of transparent objects in the layer order.

If you need to flatten your document as part of the export or print process, for best results set the document's transparency blend space (Edit > Transparency Blend Space) to the color space (CMYK or RGB) of the target output device. For more information about working with transparency see "Best practices when creating transparency" in InDesign Help.

Checking the effective resolution of linked images

You can use the Links panel to verify that the linked images have a high enough resolution for your intended mode of output. The effective resolution of a placed image is defined by the resolution of the original image and the scale factor at which it is placed in InDesign. For example, an image with a 300 ppi (pixels per inch) resolution only has an effective resolution of 150 ppi when it's scaled to 200%.

For images to be viewed at screen resolution—published on a website or in a low-resolution PDF document, for example—an effective resolution of 72 ppi is sufficient. For general office printing, the effective resolution should be between 72 ppi and 150 ppi. For commercial printing, your images should have an effective resolution between 150 ppi and 300 ppi (or higher), depending on the requirements of your prepress service provider.

1   In InDesign open the Links panel. Choose Panel Options from the Links panel menu. In the Panel Options dialog box, select the Actual PPI, Effective PPI, and Scale options in the Show column. Click OK to close the Panel Options dialog box. If necessary, resize the Links panel so that you can see the additional columns.

2   For each image placed in your document, check the actual resolution, the effective resolution, and the scale factor. For example, the cover image on page 1 has an actual resolution of 150 ppi but an effective resolution of 153 ppi because it was scaled by 98.2%. If a higher effective resolution is required for your print job, you could reduce the scale factor, which would show more of the image background, reduce the dimensions of the placed image—not really an option for the cover photo, which needs to cover the entire page—or select an image with a higher actual resolution—perhaps a close-up photo of the face rather than the wider shot that is used in this example.

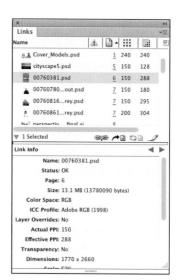

3   Close the Links panel.

Performing a preflight check

Rather than painstakingly checking through a list of possible problem areas each time you want to print or export a document, you can rely on InDesign to do all the work for you.

1 Choose Window > Output > Preflight. When the On check box is selected in the Preflight panel, InDesign continuously checks for possible problems while you're working on your document.

You can set up a preflight profile to specify which potential problems you want InDesign to look out for.

2 To define a preflight profile, choose Define Profiles from the Preflight panel options menu or from the Preflight menu located near the lower-left corner of the document window.

3 In the Preflight Profiles dialog box, click the Add button (🐾) below the list of profiles to create a new profile. Name the new profile **Resolution Check**. Activate the Image Resolution option inside the IMAGES and OBJECTS folder. Leave the Image Color Minimal Resolution set at 250 ppi, and then click OK.

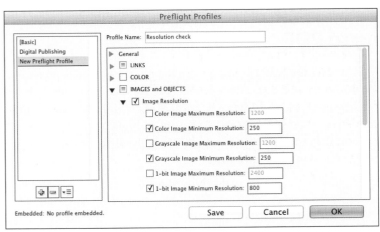

4 From the Profile menu in the Preflight panel, choose Resolution Check. If necessary, click the disclosure triangles next to the IMAGES and OBJECTS heading and the Info heading to expand their lists. InDesign finds several placed images that don't meet the set requirements. To review an error found by the Preflight check, click the page link in the Preflight panel. InDesign selects and jumps to the object causing the error. A description of the error and suggestions on how to fix the problem are provided in the Info section of the Preflight panel.

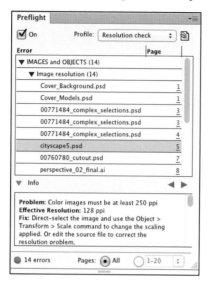

5 Switch back to the previous preflight profile by choosing [Basic] from the Profile menu in the Preflight panel, and then close the Preflight panel.

6 Save your document.

Exporting to PDF

Exporting your document as a PDF file enables you to preserve the look and feel of your InDesign document in a device-independent format that can be viewed onscreen or printed on any printer. This can be particularly useful when you want to print a quick draft of your document on an inkjet printer at home or in your office. You can tweak the export settings, balancing quality and file size to create a PDF that is optimized to suit its intended purpose.

1 Choose File > Export. In the Export dialog box, navigate to the Lesson02 folder. From the Save As Type/Format menu, choose Adobe PDF Print; name the file **Magazine_Print.pdf** and click Save.

2 In the Export Adobe PDF dialog box, choose [High Quality Print] from the Adobe PDF Preset menu. Review—but don't change—the settings for this export preset in the various panels of the dialog box, and then click Export.

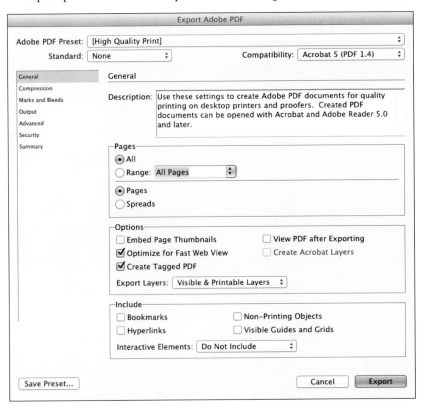

3 Open the Lesson02 folder in Windows Explorer/the Finder. Right-click/Control-click the file Magazine_Print.pdf, and choose Open With > Adobe Acrobat Pro.

4 Use the page navigation controls in Acrobat to review the pages of the magazine. Pay special attention to the position and quality of the images you placed, the text styles you've adjusted, and the areas containing transparency effects.

5 When you're done reviewing, close the document in Acrobat and switch back to InDesign.

6 Close the InDesign document, and if you're asked if you want to save changes, click Save.

Review questions

1   How can you select a frame that is stacked behind another in an InDesign document?

2   How do you edit a page so that it's a different size than the rest of the document?

3   What is a layer comp?

4   What is the effective resolution of an image placed in InDesign?

5   What is the advantage of creating a preflight profile?

Review answers

1 To select a frame that is stacked behind another frame, hold down the Ctrl/Command key, and then click inside the frame you want to select. With multiple overlapping frames, you may need to click repeatedly until the correct frame is selected. You can also select the topmost frame, and then choose Object > Select > Next Object Below.

2 With the Page tool, select the page you want to modify, and then edit the page dimensions in the Control panel.

3 A layer comp is a snapshot of the visibility settings of layers in a Photoshop document that can be used to organize multiple versions of a design in a single document. When placed in InDesign, you can quickly switch between the layer comps using the Object Layer Options dialog box.

4 The effective resolution of a placed image is defined by the actual resolution of the original image and the scale factor when placed in InDesign. For example, an image with a 300 ppi (pixels per inch) resolution has an effective resolution of only 150 ppi when scaled to 200%. Documents intended for print require images with a higher effective resolution than documents to be viewed only onscreen.

5 A preflight profile represents the output requirements of a specific job. When you create your own preflight profile that's tailored to the requirements of your print service provider, InDesign can continuously check the state of the document and its assets, and alert you to any problems that may cause an issue at output time. Because problems at output time can be expensive to fix, catching problems early can save you time and money.

3 DESIGNING FOR MOBILE DEVICES

Lesson Overview

In this lesson, you'll learn about these concepts and strategies for designing websites for mobile devices:

- Creating designs that adapt to different screen sizes by using Dreamweaver CSS Fluid Grids

- Designing with themes for mobile devices by using jQuery Mobile

- Building apps for multiple platforms by using the PhoneGap Build service

 This lesson will take about 45 minutes to complete.

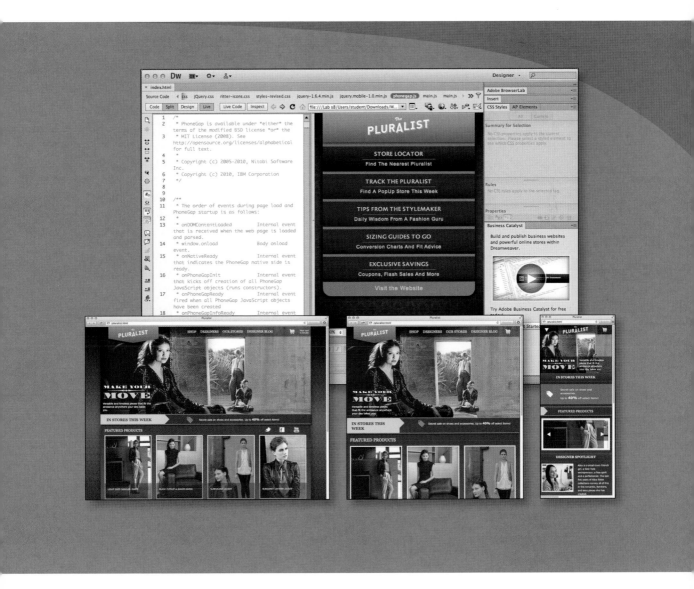

Mobile devices come in a wide range of shapes and sizes. Adobe Creative Suite 6 Design & Web Premium provides cutting-edge web design tools and support for the latest mobile design technologies to help you design for the most devices with the least effort.

New Tools for New Design Challenges

The World Wide Web was born on a desktop-sized computer screen, and although desktop and laptop computers do vary in size, with every year at least they varied in the same direction: screen sizes always got bigger. That all changed with the arrival of the smartphone, which brought back screen sizes that web designers had not seen since the early days of computing, with screens as small as 480 by 320 pixels. In addition to the new range of sizes, mobile devices used different web browsers with varying levels of support for HTML and CSS. Smartphones also brought about the touch interface, which introduced new design constraints and new opportunities, such as gestures. More recently, the new class of tablet mobile devices emerged, adding more variation to a web designer's test matrix. Together, all these challenges made designing for the mobile web a daunting task.

It's easier to design for the mobile web today because the community has taken up the challenge by developing new tools and services that greatly simplify and automate the tasks required to create websites for mobile devices. Adobe CS6 Design & Web Premium embodies many of these tools and services, tying them directly into designer-friendly applications, such as Adobe Dreamweaver.

This lesson introduces you to three solutions in Adobe CS6 Design & Web Premium that directly address three of the major challenges facing designers who create sites for the mobile web:

- Dreamweaver CSS Fluid Grids provide a way to design one site that automatically adapts to multiple screen sizes, so you don't have to create and maintain multiple site designs.

- jQuery Mobile provides a versatile toolkit for mobile design that includes button sets, mobile templates, and code hinting, so you don't have to design mobile sites from scratch.

- PhoneGap Build streamlines the process of building mobile sites to web standards, gaining access to native application programming interfaces (APIs), and building mobile apps for multiple device platforms.

As a designer, you may not directly use jQuery Mobile or PhoneGap, but when you communicate with a web developer, it's important to be aware of these solutions and what they can do for your project.

Responsive Web Layouts with Dreamweaver CSS Fluid Grids

Websites designed for a standard, desktop monitor size often appear too small on a mobile device. A popular practice has been to design an additional, separate website optimized for mobile devices. By taking advantage of CSS, it's possible to maintain a single base of content and format it differently depending on the browser that's detected. But this still requires you to work out fixed designs for each targeted device.

Now designers can take advantage of *responsive web design*. With a responsive design, elements of a web page layout can resize and dynamically rearrange based on the size and proportions of the browser window. For example, many responsive sites display as multiple columns in a large window, and as you reduce the size of the window, the layout becomes a single column. The content formerly in the right column appears at the bottom of the page. This makes it possible for the site to consist of just one design as well as just one set of content.

▶ **Tip:** Responsive web design is made possible in part by CSS Media Queries, which let your CSS code determine certain characteristics of the display device, such as resolution and aspect ratio.

As a web browser window is resized to be narrower, this responsive web layout automatically scales down images and rearranges elements from a four-column design to three columns (such as on a tablet in landscape mode) and then just one column (such as on a smartphone).

CSS Fluid Grids in Adobe Dreamweaver make it possible to create just one design that works on any device. While fluid grids are an existing CSS programming technique, with Dreamweaver CSS Fluid Grids you can design responsive websites without writing code.

You'll work with CSS Fluid Grids in Lesson 5.

▶ **Tip:** CSS Fluid Grids are based on the traditional typographic grid, which defines a page using the column as a structural unit. For example, a page might be designed around a Fluid Grid that's seven columns across.

Designing Faster with jQuery Mobile

Designing interactions and customer user interfaces has traditionally required knowing how to program in JavaScript. jQuery Mobile simplifies these tasks for designers by using syntax similar to CSS: A function can often take fewer lines of code than in JavaScript. An active community is also adding features to jQuery in the form of plug-ins.

▶ **Tip:** You can use Adobe Fireworks CS6 to create custom themes for jQuery Mobile.

To help designers realize these advantages, Adobe Dreamweaver CS6 provides support for jQuery Mobile. In Adobe Dreamweaver CS6 you can work directly with jQuery templates and themes within the application, and if you edit the code, Dreamweaver offers suggestions in the form of code hints, as it does for other markup and programming languages: As you type, Dreamweaver suggests the next bit of code that could be inserted.

jQuery Mobile provides you with templates, which are complete mobile-optimized layouts, and themes that let you easily apply a particular appearance to specific interface elements, such as buttons.

Let's try using jQuery Mobile in Dreamweaver CS6.

1   In Dreamweaver CS6, choose File > New.

2   In the New Document dialog that appears, select Page from Sample, select Mobile Starters, select jQuery Mobile (Local), and then click Create.

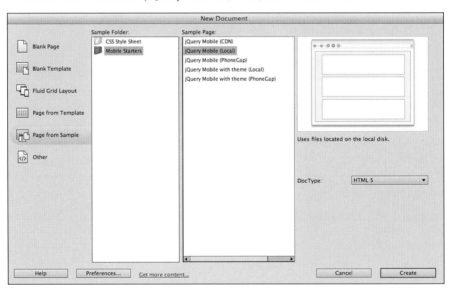

3   Choose File > Save, navigate to your Lesson03 folder, name the file
    jquery_mobile.html, and then click Save.

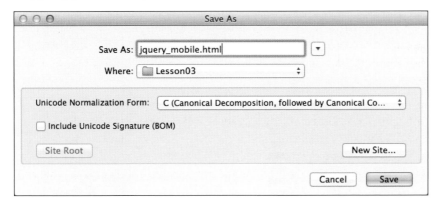

4   In the Copy Dependent Files dialog box that appears, click Copy to save the
    files to your site.

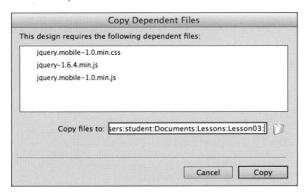

The document window displays the template content, which you can use
as a starting point.

5   Click the Split button to see the Code and Design views side by side.

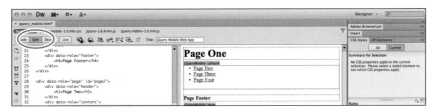

6   Select the text within the Page Two heading, and then choose Insert > jQuery Mobile > Collapsible Block.

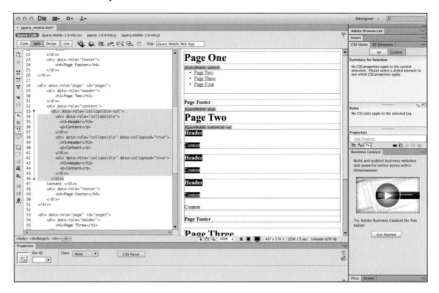

7   Click the Live button (to the right of the Code, Split, and Design buttons) to turn on Live view, which simulates how the content would look in a web browser. Click Page Two and then click the first header under Page Two to preview how the collapsible set behaves.

8 Choose Window > jQuery Mobile Swatches to open the jQuery Mobile Swatches panel.

9 Click the Live button to turn off Live view, and then in Design view (the right side of the split document window), click the Page One header text. In the Tag Selector at the bottom of the document window, click the <div> tag to select the div container that surrounds the header text.

10 Click one of the Element Theme (Header) swatches in the jQuery Mobile Swatches panel to apply formatting to the selected element.

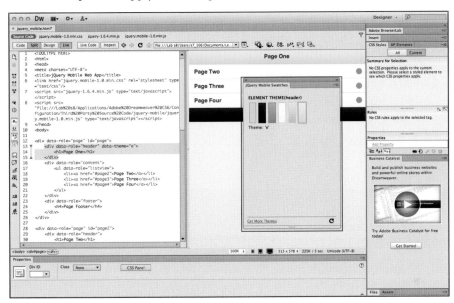

You just created a new document from a jQuery Mobile template, added a new jQuery Mobile element, and used a jQuery Mobile theme to customize the appearance of a template. After just a few clicks, you're already well on your way to creating a mobile device application!

11 Close the JQuery Mobile Swatches panel and the jquery_mobile.html document; if you're asked to save changes, click Save.

Creating Apps for Multiple Devices
with PhoneGap Build

You can use Adobe Dreamweaver CS6 to design not only mobile websites, but also mobile apps. But even after overcoming the design and coding challenges posed by the mobile web, you still need to find a practical way to create apps that run natively on every platform you want to support. Adhering to standards and accounting for the quirks of different platforms is hard enough for desktop computers, but this challenge is multiplied greatly when you consider the sheer number of mobile device models currently available.

This is where PhoneGap Build service comes into play. With PhoneGap, you don't have to manually customize your app for each platform, and you don't even have to learn how to code for each platform. You develop one version of your app using standard HTML, CSS, and JavaScript, upload your app to PhoneGap Build, and PhoneGap Build generates apps that are optimized for Android, iOS, Blackberry, WebOS, and Symbian platforms. Apps generated by PhoneGap are ready to test and ready to upload to app stores. You can also generate builds with debug code in them for testing.

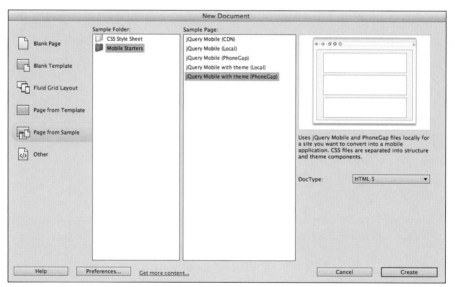

In the same New Document dialog box where you started a jQuery Mobile template, you can also select jQuery Mobile with theme (PhoneGap).

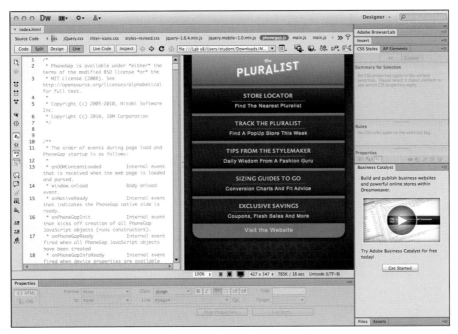

In this completed mobile application created using a PhoneGap template, the PhoneGap script is displayed in Code view.

PhoneGap Build also lets you add mobile-specific features to your app, such as support for multitouch, geolocation, and accelerometers. Your PhoneGap account (required to use PhoneGap Build) stores your development details as well as builds of your apps.

Because PhoneGap Build is largely developer-oriented, not design-oriented, it isn't covered step by step in this book.

Wrapping Up

Together, Dreamweaver CSS Fluid Grids, jQuery support, and support for PhoneGap Build greatly simplify the process of designing websites for the ever-growing diversity of mobile devices. Being aware of these features and using them when practical can help you reduce the time and effort required to publish an app.

This lesson has focused on general-purpose mobile sites and apps, but with Adobe CS6 Design & Web Premium, you also have the tools you need to design and build visually rich publications for mobile devices, such as magazine apps, as well as long documents in the form of EPUBs for mobile e-readers. You'll work with those workflows in Lesson 4.

Review questions

1 What are three challenges faced by designers of mobile websites?

2 Why are the use of Dreamweaver CSS Fluid Grids better than other ways of designing different layouts for desktop and mobile sites?

3 What are the advantages of using jQuery Mobile?

4 What are the advantages of using PhoneGap Build?

Review answers

1 The three challenges are designing for multiple screen sizes; incorporating mobile features, such as gestures, location, and accelerometers; and efficiently building native apps for a wide range of mobile devices.

2 Dreamweaver CSS Fluid Grids use responsive web design, which lets you maintain just one set of content and one design for any screen size.

3 With jQuery Mobile, you can use mobile site templates and themes to get started quickly. You also use a language that's simpler and often requires fewer lines of code than JavaScript. Code hints in Dreamweaver CS6 suggest code as you write. jQuery is also supported by an active community that develops tools, such as plug-ins and themes, that you can use.

4 With PhoneGap Build, you don't have to learn how to code for each mobile platform. You simply develop your app in HTML, CSS, and JavaScript, upload the app to PhoneGap Build, and your apps will be optimized for the mobile platforms you chose.

4 CREATING MOBILE VERSIONS OF A PRINT LAYOUT

Lesson Overview

In this lesson you'll learn key skills and techniques that will help you convert a printed brochure to a mobile format:

- Adding animation
- Adding interactivity
- Editing movie files in Adobe Photoshop
- Adding video
- Creating alternate layouts for different screen sizes
- Exporting to iPad and EPUB formats

 You'll probably need between one and two hours to complete this lesson.

Learn how to use Adobe InDesign CS6 to adapt
your print content for mobile media. Prepare video
and online media, add them and other interactive
elements to the document, and then export it as an
iPad magazine and an EPUB eBook.

Note: Before you start working on this lesson, make sure that you've installed the Creative Suite 6 software on your computer and that you have correctly copied the Lessons folder from the DVD in the back of this book onto your computer's hard drive (see "Copying the Classroom in a Book files" on page 3).

Mobile Publishing with Adobe InDesign

In Lesson 3, you learned how the latest web technologies help web designers and developers create designs that adapt to different screen sizes, screen shapes, and device hardware when building a website from scratch with HTML, CSS, and JavaScript. When you start from a print-oriented Adobe InDesign publication and you want to adapt it for viewing as an EPUB for eBooks or as a magazine-style app on a tablet, such as iPad, it's a different situation. Designing for print publications and desktop websites has traditionally assumed one target layout. As with websites, the way forward with EPUBs and tablet apps is to have a way of making a publication available in layouts that fit a range of screens and devices.

Many publications start from a print perspective because print design is so mature that it's where the most creative layouts and advanced typography is possible. When starting from a print publication and moving to mobile devices, a complicating factor is that HTML, CSS, and JavaScript cannot handle all of the design and typography features that are available in print. When preserving the sophistication of a print layout is very important, InDesign offers a powerful range of tools and options for adapting the content, such as alternate layouts, layout rules, the Content Collector, and linked content. You'll explore these later in this lesson.

Converting a Print Publication to EPUB Format

In this lesson, you'll put the finishing touches on a promotional booklet, export the document as an EPUB, and then preview the exported document.

Because electronic publications are fundamentally different than print publications in several key ways, some basic information about EPUBs may help as you work through this lesson.

The EPUB standard was designed to let publishers create reflowable content that can be displayed on any electronic reading device and software that supports the EPUB format, such as the Barnes & Noble Nook, Kobo eReader, Apple's iBooks for iPad, iPhone, Sony Reader, and Adobe Digital Editions software. Because the size of e-reader screens varies from device to device and content flows in a single, continuous thread, the page size of the InDesign document doesn't have to correspond to any particular screen size. Therefore, the fact that the document starts out at 7.5 inches by 10 inches is purely due to its original print page size, not because of any EPUB requirements.

Also, the current EPUB format does not accommodate highly designed layouts; it is primarily designed for a single text story, such as the chapter of a novel. Each page of creatively composed graphics in the sample publication will need to be exported as a single rasterized image.

Install Adobe Digital Editions

To be able to read the EPUB format documents you'll produce during this lesson, Adobe Digital Editions software must be installed on your computer. You can use Adobe Digital Editions software to download and purchase eBooks and other digital content and read them both online and offline. You can also highlight text and add comments, as well as borrow eBooks from libraries.

1 Using your web browser, go to www.adobe.com/products/digitaleditions.

2 On the web page, click the Launch button for Adobe Digital Editions Installer.

3 Follow the installation instructions. At the end, you'll be asked to activate the Adobe Digital Editions software. This is optional but recommended.

Open the sample document

In this lesson, you'll convert the same print-oriented InDesign document to more than one output format. So that you can easily start from scratch for each part of the lesson, the sample InDesign document is saved as a template.

1 Start InDesign. To ensure that the panels and menu commands match those used in this lesson, choose Window > Workspace > [Advanced], and then choose Window > Workspace > Reset Advanced. To begin working, you'll open an InDesign document that is already partially completed.

2 Open the Lesson04 folder in your Lessons folder, and double-click the file Print.indt.

3   Choose File > Save As, and save the document into your Lesson04 folder as **Pluralist.indd**. If you find the guides distracting, press W to switch to Document Preview mode.

You can see that this is a highly designed, print-oriented document that includes several double-page spreads. The EPUB format is not set up to accommodate the level of design in this document. You'll export an EPUB version of the current document to observe this.

4   Choose File > Export. Navigate into the EPUB Exported folder in your Lesson04 folder, choose EPUB from the Format menu, and click Save.

5   In the EPUB Export Options dialog box, make sure View EPUB After Exporting is selected, leave the rest of the options at their default settings, and click OK. The EPUB document opens in Adobe Digital Editions.

▶ **Tip:** If the EPUB opens in an application other than Adobe Digital Editions, close that application, start Adobe Digital Editions, choose Library > Add to Library, and then locate and double-click the EPUB file you exported in step 4.

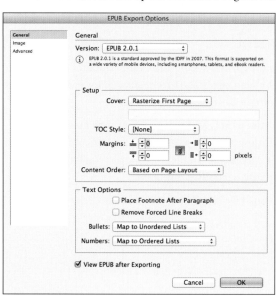

6 Scroll through the document.

You will naturally find it disappointing. The layers of objects and images appear in sequence instead, destroying all of the carefully composed layouts. The only part that seems to display correctly is the long article of text, which is what the EPUB format is optimized for.

7 Return to your Pluralist.indd document in InDesign and choose File > Save.

Preparing page layouts for the EPUB format

To include the highly graphical pages, you'll have to set them up to be rasterized at export time. Any pages that primarily consist of imported and graphic objects must be grouped into a single object and then set up for rasterization. In particular, you should redesign the double-page spreads as single vertical pages.

1 In the Pluralist.indd document, choose File > Document Setup. Set the Intent to Digital Publishing, set the Page Size to Kindle Fire/Nook, set the Orientation icon to Portrait, and click OK.

● **Note:** Setting the Document Intent to Digital Publishing automatically turns off Facing Pages.

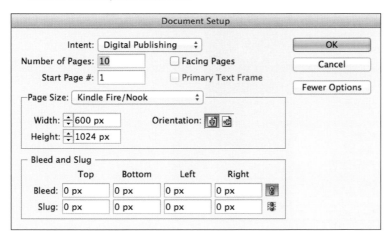

2   Choose Allow Document Pages to Shuffle from the Pages panel menu. If an alert asks you if you want to maintain the number of pages on each spread, click No. All spreads should now be single pages.

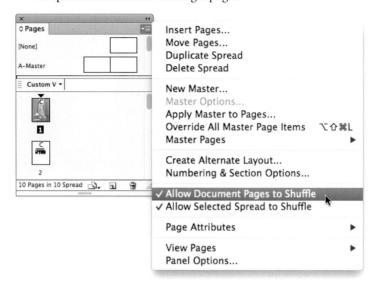

3   With the Selection tool, drag a selection marquee around all of the objects on page 1, and choose Object > Group.

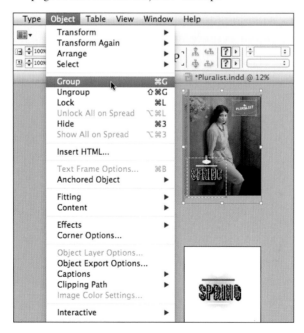

4   With the group still selected, choose Object > Object Export Options.

Online publishing with the EPUB format

The rise of eBook readers brought about the need for a standard format optimized for onscreen reading. A format that performs this role is EPUB, a digital version of a conventional printed book. The EPUB format is a free, open eBook standard. EPUB files can be read on a diverse range of eBook readers—from handheld devices (like the Sony Reader and Barnes & Noble Nook) to reading applications for desktops, tablets, and smartphones.

The EPUB format is an XML-based format designed to enable text to reflow according to the capabilities of various eBook readers, which means that you can resize the text, change the font, or view an eBook on different screen sizes, and the text will reflow to fill the available view area. This makes the EPUB format the best choice for eBooks that are read on small, handheld reading devices. In contrast, the PDF format preserves the original layout of a document, giving you complete control over page design and presentation. PDF is the optimal choice for eBooks that have a complex design or will only be read on regular-sized computer screens.

Because EPUB is XML-based, the format can be converted into other proprietary formats, such as the MOBI format, which is compatible with the Amazon Kindle. For detailed instructions on converting InDesign documents for the Kindle, see the links on the web page http://www.adobe.com/devnet/digitalpublishing/articles/indesigntokindle.html.

The EPUB format does not define page structure, so all the content flows together in one continuous, linear stream. This can present a problem for publications that have an elaborate design. If your layout is quite simple, you probably won't notice much of a difference between it and its eBook equivalent. Because the EPUB format is based on XML, which is similar to the CSS web standard, the more a publication is formatted similarly to a CSS layout, the higher the chance that the document will translate well to EPUB.

Some publications may be too design-intensive to be properly presented as an EPUB file. In such cases, PDF is a more suitable format for online viewing.

InDesign CS6 can export directly to the EPUB format; just choose File > Export for > EPUB. In the EPUB Export Options dialog box, you can specify how formatting in the InDesign file will be translated to the EPUB format.

To preview your EPUB documents, use Adobe Digital Editions software, which is a free download from adobe.com.

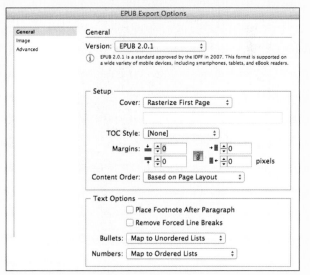

5 In the Object Export Options dialog box, click the EPUB and HTML tab, and select Custom Rasterization. For Resolution (ppi), choose 150. Leave the other settings as they are, and click Done.

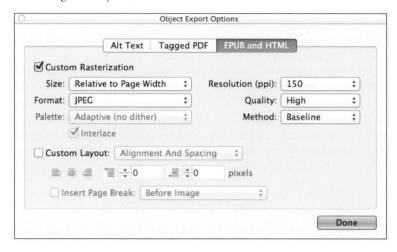

▶ **Tip:** If some of the grouped objects export to EPUB as separate objects, make sure you have grouped all objects on the page and properly set the Object Export Options to rasterize the group.

6 Drag the Spring type from page 2 to page 3, and compose it with the photo on page 3. When you're done, group everything on page 3 as you did in step 3.

7 Set the Object Export Options for the group on page 3, as you did in steps 4 and 5.

8 Recompose the objects on page 4 and 5 to fit on page 4 only. You can scale down the Beauty text.

9 For page 4, repeat steps 3 through 5 to create one group out of all the objects on the page.

10 Use the Pages panel to delete the empty pages 2 and 5.

11 On pages 5 and 6, delete all objects except the two-column text frame. Leaving only the text frame allows it to flow as a single text story, which is the optimum design for an EPUB document because it doesn't rasterize the text.

12 If you didn't delete the "A" drop cap, delete it now, because the graphic drop cap won't translate to EPUB format.

13 Then, using the Type tool, click an insertion point at the beginning of the two-column text frame and type a capital A to replace the drop cap.

14 Open the Paragraph Styles panel (Window > Styles > Paragraph Styles), and choose Edit All Export Tags from the Paragraph Styles panel menu.

EPUB is based on HTML, so for compatibility with the widest selection of e-readers, it's a good idea to map publication styles to HTML CSS styles.

15 For the style Print_BODY, click Automatic in the Tag column; then click the arrows to see the style choices, and choose p. Click OK.

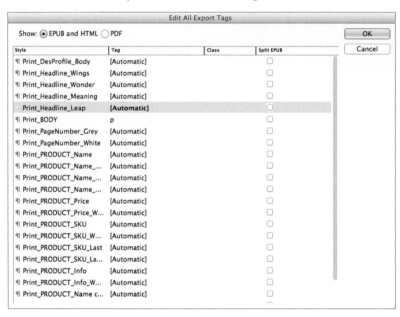

Tip: The Split EPUB option you see in the Edit All Export Tags dialog box is a way to insert a page break before specific paragraph styles. You may want to do this to control pagination and make long documents easier to navigate. However, this option results in a higher number of files in the EPUB package.

This particular document isn't text-heavy, but if it was, mapping the rest of the styles to standard HTML CSS styles would make a more noticeable visual difference. In addition, you'd be able to define styles that set page breaks, and then apply those styles to headings or inline graphics to mark the beginning of each page.

Adding metadata

When an EPUB document is listed in an e-reader or other database, the information that's visible is taken from the metadata for the file. It's a good idea to customize that information.

1 Choose File > File Info.

2 For Document Title, type **Pluralist**. For Author, type your name.

Note that the rest of the dialog box gives you an opportunity to enter detailed descriptive text, including a copyright notice.

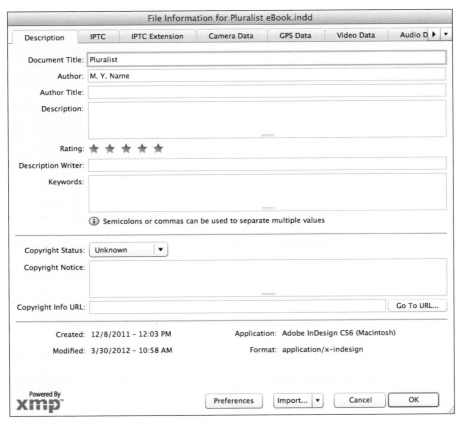

3 Click OK.

Understanding More Details
About Exporting to EPUB

Now it's time to export the document again, to see whether the settings you changed will result in a better EPUB document than the one you exported earlier.

1 Choose File > Export. Navigate into the EPUB Exported folder in your Lesson04 folder, choose EPUB from the Format menu, and click Save without changing the filename. Click Replace when asked if you want to replace the existing document.

2 In the EPUB Export Options dialog box that appears, make sure View EPUB After Exporting is selected.

Although many of the EPUB export options can remain at their default settings, you may consider adjusting the following:

- In the General pane under the Text Options section, it's a good idea to select Map to Unordered Lists in the Bullets menu and select Map to Ordered Lists in the Numbers menu.

- In the Image pane, make sure Preserve Appearance from Layout is selected to maintain image cropping and settings.

- In the Advanced pane, leave all the check boxes selected to help preserve the original appearance of the document.

Note: Not all e-readers support font embedding. If possible, test your EPUB on various devices to ensure that you're satisfied with the output.

Note: InDesign automatically generates a Unique ID for an EPUB; however, for commercial EPUBs, you would enter the ISBN.

Note: By default, items on a page that was originally designed for print may not appear in an ideal order when exported to EPUB format. For more control over the reading order and the relationships among page items, arrange them in the Articles panel (Window > Articles).

3 Click OK. The EPUB document opens in Adobe Digital Editions.

The result this time should look much better, resolving the issues seen after the previous time you exported to EPUB. If you were to design an EPUB document from scratch, you would design it as one, long, text story with full-page layouts consolidated into single, rasterized graphics.

4 Exit Adobe Digital Editions, and in InDesign close the document Pluralist.indd.

● **Note:** By default, hyperlinks open in an in-app Viewer, not in Safari. You can use the Folio Overlays panel to change the settings of a hyperlink to Open In Device Browser so that it opens a website in Safari.

Creating a Video with Photoshop

When you move a publication from paper to mobile devices, you introduce the possibility of adding media, such as a video, that you couldn't use in a printed piece. Video is now easy to capture using most mobile devices, easy to edit on almost any new computer, and easy to distribute over broadband networks. Consistent with these trends, the video-editing features that were once included only in Adobe Photoshop Extended are now in the Standard edition of Adobe Photoshop CS6. .

You'll use Photoshop to create an animated piece that's included in an iPad publication you'll build later in this lesson.

1 Start Adobe Photoshop CS6.

2 Choose Window > Workspace > Essentials (Default), and then choose Window > Workspace > Reset Essentials.

3 Choose File > New. From the Preset menu, choose Film & Video. For Size choose HD/HDTV 720p/29.97. For Name, type **Ritter**, and click OK. If you see a pixel aspect ratio warning, click OK.

● **Note:** The video-editing features in Photoshop CS6 are not meant to replace the full power of a professional, video-editing application, such as Adobe Premiere Pro CS6 (which is not included in Adobe CS6 Design & Web Premium). Instead, the video tools in Photoshop are intended to let designers easily work with video and include it in design projects

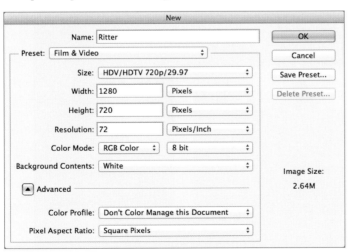

4 Click the Mini Bridge tab at the bottom of the workspace to expand the panel, and then click Launch Bridge. (If you don't see a Mini Bridge tab, choose Window > Mini Bridge.)

5 Use Mini Bridge to locate and select the folder Links in your Lesson04 folder. Images should appear in Mini Bridge.

6 Click the Sort icon, and make sure it's set to sort by filename.

7 Select the first three photo thumbnails in Mini Bridge (not including the sketches), and drag them into the document.

8 When the first image appears in the document, press Enter to place it in the document as a Smart Object. Continue pressing Enter until all images are placed.

9 Click the Timeline tab to reveal the Timeline panel, and then click Create Video Timeline. Photoshop creates a video timeline of all layers in the document; the timeline is five seconds long by default. Drag the top edge of the Timeline panel so you can see all of the layers.

10 In the Layers panel or the Timeline panel, Shift-select all three photo layers, and then with the Move tool, Shift-drag all selected layers to the left until they are offscreen.

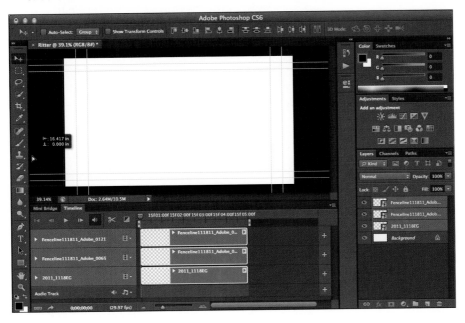

11 Choose Select > Deselect Layers.

12 In the Timeline panel, click the disclosure triangle to the left of the bottom layer, 2011_1118EG. Click the icon for the Transform property to enable it, adding yellow keyframe markers to the Timeline.

13 Drag the blue current-time indicator to the 1-second mark on the Timeline.

14 With the Move tool, drag layer 2011_1118EG until the sitting model's boots are just inside the action-safe guides.

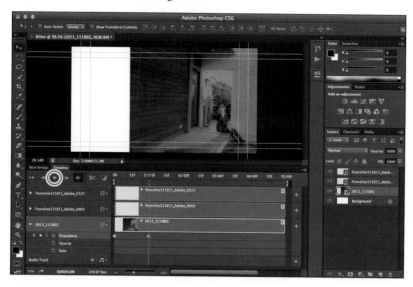

15 Move the current-time indicator to the beginning of the Timeline, and click Play. The two keyframes you set control the start and end of the layer animation.

16 Select the middle layer in the Timeline. Repeat steps 11 through 13, but this time set the starting keyframe at 1 second and the ending keyframe at 2 seconds, and stop the image before it overlaps the left model in the bottom layer.

17 Select the top layer in the Timeline. Repeat steps 11 through 13, but this time set the starting keyframe at 2 seconds and the ending keyframe at 3 seconds, and stop the image as soon as it's aligned with the left edge of the frame.

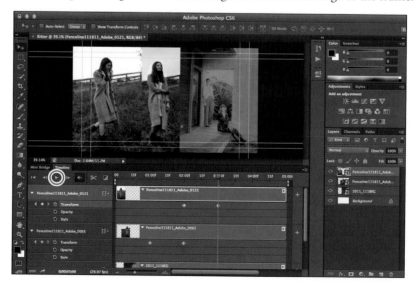

18 Return the current-time indicator to the beginning of the Timeline, and click Play. The three layers should appear in turn, filling the frame from right to left.

Render the timeline to a final video file

Up until now, the video exists only as objects on a timeline. When you're done editing, you need to export the timeline into a video format that's appropriate for your purposes. Because you plan to use this video as part of a mobile application, you'll use the H.264 format.

1 Choose Render Video from the Timeline panel menu.

2 In the Render Video dialog box, click Select Folder and navigate to the Links folder in the Lesson04 folder.

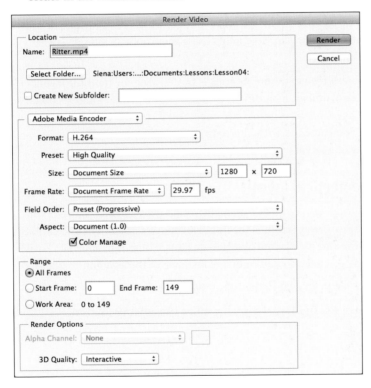

3 Make sure Adobe Media Encoder and the H.264 format are selected; click Select Folder, navigate to the Lesson04 folder and click Choose, and then click Render.

4 When rendering is complete, double-click the Ritter.mp4 video file to view it.

Of course, this is just a taste of the Timeline because you're not limited to working with stills. You can also edit video clips in the Timeline, add text layers, and add audio, and none of these tasks are more difficult than animating stills, as you just did.

Converting a Print Publication to an iPad App Using InDesign

Earlier you adjusted a layout for export to the EPUB format, and in the process you learned about the limitations of EPUB. When you want to preserve more layout flexibility and distribute your publication on tablets, such as the Apple iPad, you can create a mobile app from an InDesign document with the help of the Adobe Digital Publishing Suite (DPS). The advantage of using the DPS app over the EPUB format is that you use the advanced layout capabilities of HTML5 when rendering through WebKit-based browsers, which means you can more easily execute sophisticated designs and rasterize entire pages less often. The DPS mobile app is more appropriate for a magazine-style layout.

When you create a DPS publication, you create a folio, which contains one or more digital publishing articles. You can view folios using the Adobe Content Viewer, which comes with InDesign.

One of the ways InDesign enables mobile apps is by allowing for multiple layouts in a single InDesign document, including the ability to link primary and secondary layouts so that you have to edit content only once. You'll start by converting a print publication so that you can work with alternate layouts, such as the horizontal and vertical orientations of a tablet.

Setting up the vertical layout

To streamline the production of mobile apps, InDesign uses a primary layout and alternate layouts. The primary layout is the initial layout of a document and contains the source content for alternate layouts you create later. Content in alternate layouts can be linked so that you need to edit only one instance of the content.

1   Double-click the file Print.indt in the Lesson04 folder.

2   Choose File > Save As, and save the document as **Pluralist iPad.indd**.

3 Choose File > Document Setup, and choose Digital Publishing from the Intent menu. Make sure iPad is the selected Page Size and that the Orientation icon is set to Portrait, and click OK. Notice that the page size changes.

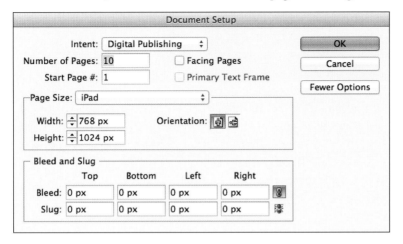

Adding interactive elements

Interactive elements in a digital publication include slide shows, hyperlinks, graphics that a viewer can pan and zoom, and movies and sounds. Much like you can modify a graphics frame by adding a stroke or a special effect like a drop shadow or rotation, you can control the appearance and function of interactive elements.

Creating hyperlinks and buttons

Hyperlinks let viewers jump to other locations in a document, as well as to other documents or websites. A hyperlink includes a source (text, a text frame, or a graphics frame) and a destination, which is the URL, file, e-mail address, page text anchor, or shared destination to which the hyperlink jumps. Next, you'll create a hyperlink to a website using an empty graphics frame.

1 Select the Rectangle Frame tool (F), and drag a rectangle around the Pluralist logo on page 1.

2 Choose Window > Interactive > Hyperlinks.

3 Choose New Hyperlink from the Hyperlinks panel menu.

4   Select URL from the Link To menu, and type a URL address in the URL field. Deselect Shared Hyperlink Destination. Under Appearance, leave Invisible Rectangle and None selected. Click OK.

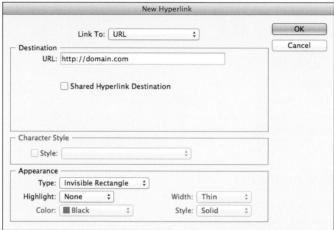

5   Choose Window > Folio Overlays, and make sure Open in Folio is selected. This will come into play when you preview the link later.

6   Choose Edit > Deselect All.

Comparing buttons and hyperlinks

You can use buttons and hyperlinks to build navigation controls in InDesign. At first glance, it might seem that there's overlap between what buttons and hyperlinks can do, so to choose between them, you need to know a few key differences in how they work.

Buttons are generally graphic in nature, such as a picture or drawn object that you set up as a button. A button works much like a graphics frame; for example, you can replace the contents of a button. Buttons can also have multiple states. Options for buttons are in the Buttons panel (Window > Interactive > Buttons). You're more likely to use buttons in graphically engaging multimedia projects where appearance and compelling interactivity is important.

Hyperlinks are generally text-based and can be generated from text. For example, InDesign can create a live URL hyperlink from URL text you've selected. Hyperlinks have fewer display and rollover options than buttons, and have only a couple of basic states. Hyperlink options are in the Hyperlinks panel (Window > Interactive > Hyperlinks). You're more likely to use hyperlinks in a text-heavy reference document where the hyperlinks may be automatically generated and also automatically preserved when you export the file to EPUB or PDF.

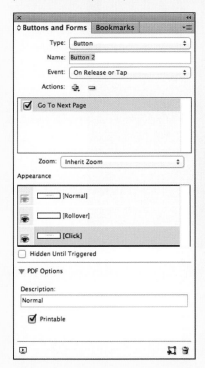

Adding a video

InDesign CS6 lets you easily add a video to a document so that it can play back on desktop and mobile devices that support video. Adding a movie to a digital publishing document is the same as adding a photo or illustration to a print document. You'll import a movie into the document and use the Media panel to choose a graphic as the poster image for the movie. Then you'll use the Folio Overlays panel to control how the movie plays.

1 Go to page 2.

2 Choose File > Place and select the Ritter.mp4 video file that you created in the Links folder in the Lesson04 folder. Click Open.

3 On page 2, drag the Place icon to create a rectangle to the right of the models, about halfway down the page, to contain the video.

4 Choose Object > Fitting > Fit Frame to Content to make the frame fit exactly the size you dragged.

5 Choose Window > Interactive > Media.

6   From the Poster menu in the Media panel, choose Choose Image. Select the
    IMG_0968.jpg in the Links folder in the Lesson04 folder, and then click Open.
    This sets the image that appears on the page when the video isn't playing.

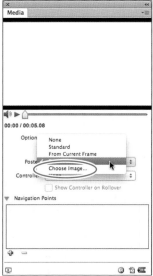

7   With the movie object still selected, make sure
    that Auto Play and Play Full Screen are not
    selected in the Folio Overlays panel, and that
    Tap To View Controller is selected.

8   Choose File > Save.

Testing interactivity

You can use the Folio Overlays panel to preview the interactive overlays you've added.

1 At the bottom of the Folio Overlays panel, click Preview.

   An alert appears warning you that only one page per spread is supported. The reason is that mobile devices typically display one page per screen. You'll need to convert all spreads to single pages, as you did for the EPUB document earlier in this lesson.

2 Choose File > Document Setup, and make sure Facing Pages is deselected. Click OK.

3 Choose Allow Document Pages to Shuffle from the Pages panel menu. If an alert asks you if you want to maintain the number of pages on each spread, click No. All spreads should now be single pages.

4 Due to the logo on page 2, which is left over from a double-page spread, page 1 and page 2 are now redundant, so in the Pages panel, drag page 2 to the trash can icon. Do the same for the empty page 4. If a warning appears, click OK.

5 At the bottom of the Folio Overlays panel, click Preview. Adobe Content Viewer starts and displays the document. Scroll through the document using the up and down arrow keys or by swiping up and down with the mouse.

6 Go to page 1 and click the logo with the link you created. It should go to the link. Click Done to return to the document.

7 Go to page 2 and click the movie you created. It should begin playing back.

Set up layout rules

The document is set up for a vertical orientation only. But a mobile app also needs a layout for a horizontal orientation. InDesign provides for this through alternate layouts and helps you adapt your layouts with Liquid Layout rules.

Each page can have its own Liquid Layout rule:

- **Scale** simply fills the new page size with the current content resized.

- **Re-center** keeps content centered within the new layout

- **An object-based rule** allows for rules that control a specific object; you can pin any corner to maintain its relationship to the edge of a page.

- **A guide-based rule** constrains page adjustment along layout guides you position.

You'll set up a combination of these rules, and then create an alternate layout based on them.

1 In InDesign, choose Layout > Liquid Layout.

2 On page 1, use the Page tool (Shift+P) to select the diagonal red stripes along the left side of the page.

3 In the Liquid Layout panel, choose Object-based, and for Pin, select Left.

4 Position the mouse over the handles on the selected object. Tool tips describe how the object will behave when the page is resized.

5 Still using the Page tool, select The Pluralist logo in the top-right corner, and in the Liquid Layout panel, choose Object-based and set the Pin options to Top and Right.

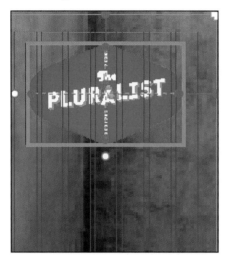

6 Select the Spring Collection logo in the bottom-left corner, and in the Liquid Layout panel, choose Object-based and set the Pin options to Bottom and Left.

7 Select the photo, and in the Liquid Layout panel, choose Object-based, and select the Auto-Fit and Width options.

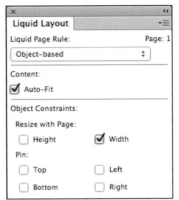

8 With the Page tool still selected, test your settings by clicking the Landscape orientation icon in the Control panel. All objects on the page that use Liquid Layout rules should reposition and resize to maintain the intended layout despite the radical change in proportions.

9 Choose Edit > Undo Resize Item to restore the original orientation.

10 Choose File > Save.

Create a horizontal layout

In programs that don't allow alternate layouts, creating a layout for a mobile device's multiple orientations typically requires creating a separate document for each orientation. In InDesign, you simply create an alternate layout that exists as a separate section in the same InDesign document. You've already set up the rules that describe how page objects translate from one orientation to the other; now you'll actually create the alternate layout for the landscape (horizontal) orientation.

1 Choose Layout > Create Alternate Layout.

2 For Page Size, choose iPad, and make sure the Orientation icon is set to landscape.

3 Click OK.

A new section appears in the document, duplicating the original pages but using a horizontal orientation. Notice how page 1 adapted well to the landscape orientation but the rest of the pages did not. The reason is that layout rules weren't applied to the rest of the pages. You can experiment with applying layout rules to achieve an optimum conversion. Alternately, you can lay out the content manually but as linked content—where the content of the alternate layout is linked to the primary layout so you only have to update the primary content.

1 Go to page 4 of the alternate (horizontal) layout section, and delete the objects on that layout. Do the same for the alternate layouts for pages 5 and 6.

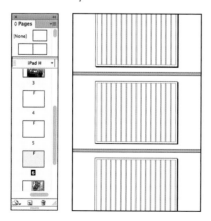

2   Go to page 4 of the primary (vertical) section, and use the Content Collector tool (B) to click the Alice and Ritter graphic headline text as well as the photo. Notice that they appear in the Content Collector conveyor.

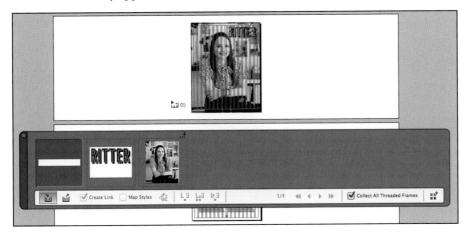

3   In the Content Collector conveyor, make sure Collect All Threaded Frames is selected; then on page 5, use the Content Collector tool to click the frame containing the threaded story.

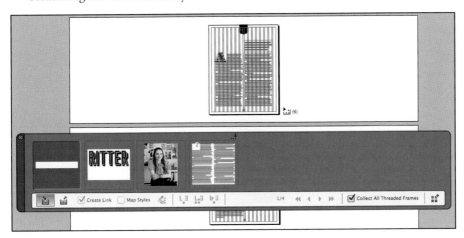

4   Go to page 4 of the alternate (horizontal) layout section.

5 In the conveyor, click the Content Placer icon and make sure Create Link is selected.

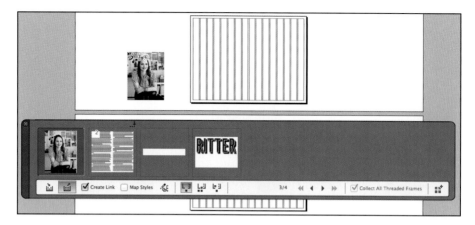

Publishing an app through a store

To be able to submit an InDesign folio as an app to a store such as the Apple App Store, there are a few more requirements that are outside the scope of this lesson. You'll need:

• An Adobe Digital Publishing Suite account (http://digitalpublishing.acrobat. com), so you can organize, edit, and publish folios with Folio Producer, and arrange articles and edit metadata with Folio Producer Editor. You can sign into Adobe Digital Publishing Suite using your Adobe ID.

• An Adobe Digital Publishing Suite Single Edition serial number to publish a single issue with a single folio, a Professional Edition subscription for unlimited custom viewer apps and folios, or an Enterprise Edition subscription for advanced customization and analytics. You can view pricing information for these options at http://www.adobe.com/products/digital-publishing-suite-family/buying-guide.html.

• Any membership required for the store where you want to submit your app. For example, submitting an app to the Apple App Store requires membership in the Apple iOS Developer Program, which involves an annual fee.

• An Internet connection so that you can interact with Adobe Digital Publishing Suite and the stores where you want to submit your app.

6 Press the left or right arrow key to cycle through the items in the loaded pointer until you see the photo. On page 4 of the horizontal layout, drag from the top-left corner to the bottom-right corner to place the image.

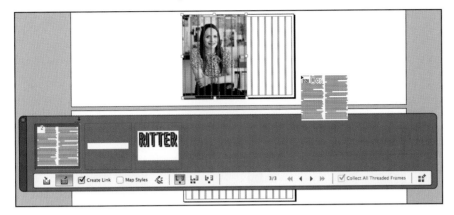

7 Drag the white Alice text over the photo and the Ritter text across the top of the right half of the page.

8 Drag the text frame across the rest of the page, and then use the Selection tool to extend its width across the page if needed.

By selecting Create Link, the content you transferred is now linked to the primary layout. If you need to edit any part of the content, you only need to do so in the primary layout; the alternate layout will update, saving you time. The Content Collector helps you transfer multiple items more efficiently than dragging and dropping or copying and pasting.

Previewing the updated document

To see how your alternate layout looks while viewing any of the pages in the landscape format section, choose File > Folio Preview.

InDesign exports the folio to Adobe Content Viewer, where you can test the document. To navigate, drag the layout up and down or press the up arrow and down arrow keys. You can use the commands on the View menu to preview other screen sizes and orientations. Remember to click the movie you added on page 2.

● **Note:** You can also preview your folio by installing Adobe Content Viewer from the App Store, starting it, and signing in using your Adobe ID.

You can share the folio file with other individuals using Folio Producer, a publishing tool available when you log into Adobe Digital Publishing Suite using your Adobe ID. If you want to be able to submit a folio as an app to a store, additional steps and fees are required; see the sidebar "Publishing an App Through a Store."

Wrapping Up

Congratulations! You've learned techniques for converting a print document into an EPUB document and an iPad app. Although manual adjustment was necessary, layout rules, mapped styles (in the Edit All Export Tags dialog box), alternate layouts, the Content Collector, and the Folio Viewer all work together to minimize the amount of rework you might have had to do otherwise, making it easier to publish mobile versions of your documents.

Review questions

1   When would you want to export an InDesign document to the EPUB format, and when would you want to export it as a mobile application?

2   In InDesign, what is the difference between a button and a hyperlink?

3   What's the difference between how you test EPUB documents and mobile applications in InDesign?

4   What is a poster image, and how do you set it?

5   What is the value of an object-based layout rule?

Review answers

1   You would export to EPUB when you want to distribute a document to ereaders and when the document is primarily text. You would export as a mobile application for more sophisticated magazine-style layouts that are beyond the capabilities of EPUB.

2   Buttons tend to be graphics, and hyperlinks are usually text-based.

3   You can test EPUB documents in Adobe Digital Editions and mobile applications in Adobe Content Viewer.

4   A poster image is the frame that represents a video in an InDesign layout. By default, the poster image is the first frame of a video, but you can change that in the Poster menu in the Media panel.

5   An object-based layout rule lets you control how an object responds to a change in page dimensions. For example, you can pin the top and left edges of a graphic to the page so that it remains at the top-left corner of the page.

5 BUILDING A WEBSITE

Lesson Overview

In this lesson, you'll learn the following skills and techniques:

- A typical Dreamweaver workflow
- Previewing website assets in Adobe Bridge
- Using fluid grid layouts to get going quickly
- Inspecting and editing CSS (Cascading Style Sheet) properties
- Placing, scaling, and adjusting images
- Previewing and adapting a website for mobile screens
- Inserting Fireworks HTML pages
- Roundtrip editing between Dreamweaver and Fireworks

 This lesson will take about two hours to complete.

Learn how to use Dreamweaver to rapidly design a website that adapts to different screen sizes without making alternate versions of the site. Minimize design time using fluid grid layouts. Add images, use roundtrip editing with Fireworks, and easily preview how your website looks on smartphones and tablets.

Designing Modern Websites

● **Note:** Before you start working on this lesson, make sure that you've installed the Creative Suite 6 software on your computer and that you have correctly copied the Lessons folder from the DVD in the back of this book onto your computer's hard drive (see "Copying the Classroom in a Book files" on page 3).

The rapid rise of mobile devices, such as smartphones and tablets, has changed the entire approach to website design. Instead of designing for a single screen resolution you expect most of your audience to use or even designing separate sites for desktop computers and mobile devices, you can now design a single site that automatically adapts to different screen sizes—this is called a *responsive layout*. Adobe Dreamweaver CS6 makes this simple with fluid grid layouts, which are easy to use because you work with them visually instead of by writing code. Dreamweaver also makes it easy to preview how your design looks on a wide range of devices.

Previewing the assets in Adobe Bridge

To get a first impression of the images you'll use in this lesson, preview the files in your Lesson05 folder using Adobe Bridge.

1 Start Adobe Bridge CS6.

2 In Adobe Bridge, navigate to the Lesson05 folder on your hard drive. At first, you see only a few folders and an HTML document. To see all of the items in every folder at once, choose View > Show Items from Subfolders.

In the following example, we started from the Essentials workspace in Adobe Bridge and arranged the panels so that the Content, Preview, and Metadata panels were visible at once. You can see that the files for this lesson include HTML documents, images in various formats, JavaScript files (the icons marked JS), and Cascading Style Sheet files (the icons marked CSS).

When you arrange the Adobe Bridge window this way, selecting a file reveals information about it in the Metadata panel, such as its pixel dimensions. The photo selected in the preceding figure is shown as 480 pixels by 633 pixels.

Designing responsive web pages using a fluid grid layout

In the following exercises you'll work on two pages of a prototype website in Adobe Dreamweaver. You'll learn how to quickly set up a web page layout that adapts to different screen sizes, and preview the design in a web browser.

1   Start Dreamweaver, and in the Welcome Screen click Fluid Grid Layout.

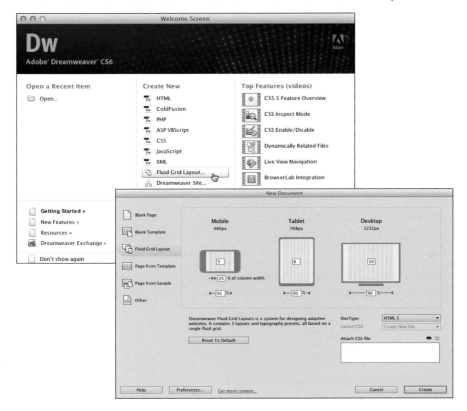

In the New Document dialog box, the number inside each screen-size graphic is the number of columns across the design, and the percentage below each graphic is the percentage of the width of the screen used for the body of the page.

Now you'll save the page for the first time. This happens in two stages: saving a CSS file and then an HTML file. The CSS file defines the page's styles and layout, whereas the HTML file describes what's included in the file. In other words, for a web page, CSS defines form and HTML defines content.

2   Leave the defaults and click Create.

3   In the Save Style Sheet File As dialog box that appears, browse to select the CSS folder inside the Lesson05 folder. With the CSS subfolder selected, name the new CSS file **fluid.css**, and click Save.

4   Choose File > Save. Name the file **fluid.html**, and save the new HTML5 file. Be sure to save it at the top level of the Lesson05 folder, alongside the CSS subfolder.

5   In the Copy Dependent Files dialog box that appears, click Copy to save the two listed files (which are required) automatically to the proper subfolder inside your Lesson05 folder.

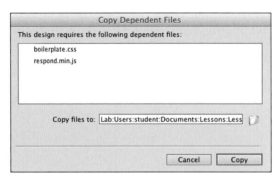

6   Click the Split button at the top left of the document window. Now you can see Code view and Design view at the same time. If you edit either view, both views update. If you prefer, you can show just the code or just the design.

7   In Design view, click inside the green default div container to select it. A *div* is a layer in an HTML page.

8   In the HTML section of the Properties inspector at the bottom of the window, select the existing div container's name in the ID field (LayoutDiv1) and rename it **Header**.

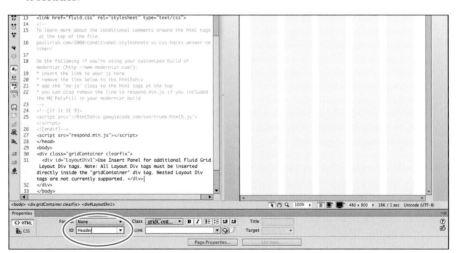

9 Click in the white space to the right of the bottom-right corner of the existing green gridContainer div element. In Code view on the left, verify that the cursor's insertion point is located after the closing </div> tag of the default gridContainer layer (at the end of code line 31).

10 In the Layout category of the Insert panel, click Insert Fluid Grid Layout Div Tag.

11 In the ID field of the Insert Fluid Grid Layout Div Tag dialog box, name the second div tag **Nav**.

Click here

Insert Fluid Grid Layout Div Tag button

12 Add four more divs by repeating steps 10 and 11, and name the new divs **Intro**, **Main**, **Aside**, and **Footer**.

At the bottom of the window is the Resolution Switcher with three icons and a pop-up menu. The three icons are presets for previewing mobile, tablet, and desktop sizes in Design view, and the pop-up menu lets you set up custom sizes. It's recommended that you start designing for the smallest screen size you want your site to support.

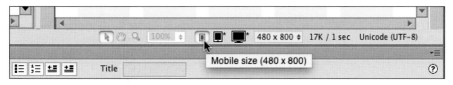

Mobile size (480 x 800)

13 In the Resolution Switcher, click the largest icon (Desktop Size) to see how the layout changes.

To the left of the Resolution Switcher is a magnification pop-up menu. It's enabled when Design view is active.

14 Click the Magnification pop-up menu and choose Fit All so that you can see the entire layout, and then click the Tablet Size and Mobile Size buttons in the Resolution Switcher to see how the current layout adjusts to each size. When you're done, choose 100% from the Magnification pop-up menu.

15 Click the Live button at the top of the document window. This changes the Design view to Live view, which previews your site using WebKit so that it accurately appears as it would on WebKit-based web browsers.

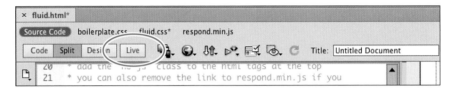

Now you can see that for a small mobile screen, the content of every layer (div) becomes a row taking up the entire width of the screen and spanning all of the columns displayed in pink.

16 Click the Tablet Size button, and as needed, adjust the width of the Design view by dragging the separator in the middle of the window so that you can see the entire width of the Tablet size at 100% magnification.

17 Select the Aside div element, and drag the handle in the middle of its right edge to make it four columns wide. Notice that the width automatically snaps to the column grid. Adjust the width of the Main layer in the same way.

18 Select the Aside layer and click the Move Up a Row button that appears to the right of the div element. Now the Main and Aside layers are on the same row, which makes sense on the greater screen width of a tablet.

19 Use the Resolution Switcher to switch between the Mobile and Tablet sizes, and view the different layouts you've assigned to each size. Feel free to experiment further with the layouts for the three sizes.

20 Close the fluid.html file, and save changes if asked.

So far you've adjusted two different layouts for mobile and tablet screen sizes. Let's see how such a design could look in finished form.

Preview a website for mobile screens

Next, you'll preview a finished layout that was built using techniques similar to those you just used. You'll locate the finished layout using the Files panel, which lets you browse files without leaving Dreamweaver. You'll also try the Multiscreen Preview, which lets you see how your site looks at multiple sizes at once.

1 In the Files panel, locate the file pluralist.html in your Lesson05 folder, and double-click it. (If you can't find the Files panel, choose Window > Files.)

2 Click the Preview/Debug in Browser button, and choose a web browser from the list.

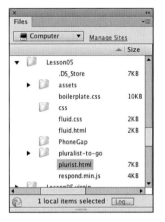

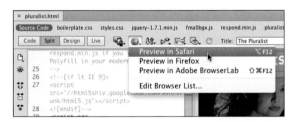

3 Resize your web browser window to see how the layout responds. Be sure to try full screen and very small, narrow window sizes to simulate desktop and mobile screens.

Notice that the layout automatically rearranges the layers to a single column for the narrowest window size.

Now that you've seen the web browser preview, you'll take a second look at the document in Dreamweaver and edit it. First you'll turn off the green Fluid Grid Layout Guides, which are useful when designing the overall layout but can get in the way when working with design details.

4 Switch to Dreamweaver, click the Visual Aids button, and then deselect the Fluid Grid Layout Guides command.

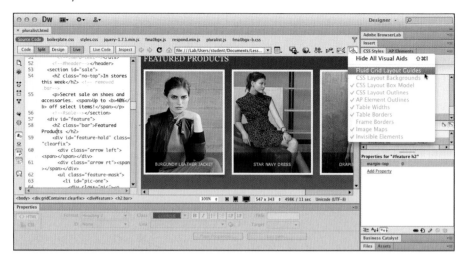

5 Make sure the Live button is on, and click the Mobile, Tablet, and Desktop buttons in the Resolution Switcher to observe how the layers were designed for each size. You can examine the layers and the code to see how it was done.

6 Click the Multiscreen button and choose the Multiscreen Preview command from the menu.

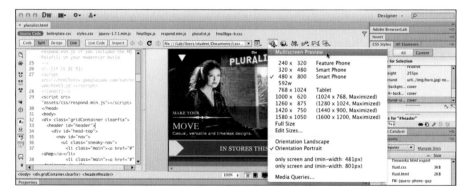

● **Note:** If you can't see the right scroll bar after enlarging a viewport, position the mouse over the right edge of the Multiscreen Preview window until you see a two-headed arrow, and then drag to the right.

The Multiscreen Preview opens, showing you Phone, Tablet, and Desktop views all at once. Each of the views is called a viewport. Use the scroll bars to preview the full height of each viewport.

7   Click the Viewport Sizes button in the top-right corner of the Multiscreen Preview window.

8   In the Viewport Sizes dialog box, for Tablet enter **1024** for Width and **768** for Height, and then click OK. This is how you can customize the size of each viewport. Many tablets have pixel dimensions of 1024 x 768 in the landscape orientation, so if the tablet audience is important to you, you may want to create a viewport of this size for previewing your website.

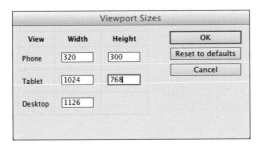

9   Move the pointer over the text at the bottom of the Featured Products section of the website in the Tablet viewport to preview the mouse-activated animations. Unfortunately you can't follow the links.

10 Click the Viewport Sizes button, click the Reset to Defaults button, and click OK. This default configuration makes it easier to fit all three viewports on one display.

11 Close the Multiscreen Preview panel.

Inspecting and Editing CSS Page Elements

Being able to work with CSS-based page elements is essential as you design a website. Dreamweaver gives you a comprehensive set of tools to help you inspect the attributes of any CSS layer in detail, and then to edit those attributes.

When you select an element such as text, a div layer, or an image, the Properties panel tells you about general CSS and HTML formatting, including the CSS Class and ID; the CSS Styles panel shows you detailed element-level information about the applied style, such as font size, margins, and positioning.

1   Turn off Live View, and in the Resolution Switcher, click the Tablet Size button. In the file pluralist.html, select any instance of the Alice Ritter uppercase text.

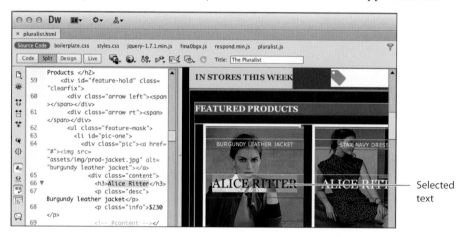

Selected text

You can learn almost anything you need to know about the selected element by looking at the panels around the document window:

- The Code view on the left highlights the code for the selected element.

- The Properties panel at the bottom of the workspace tells you that the text is Heading 3, which belongs to a div layer of the CSS class "content." If you wanted the text to be a link, you would type the link URL into the Link option in the Properties panel.

- The CSS Styles panel on the right displays all of the CSS attribute settings that are applied to the selected element. Those attributes are derived from the style rules applied, which are displayed in the Rules at the bottom of the CSS Styles panel.

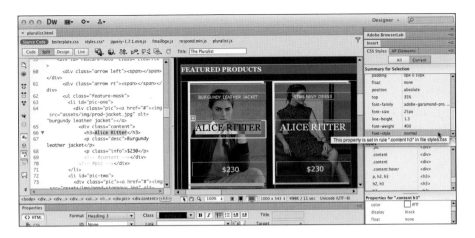

If you want to edit a CSS rule, you can do so from the CSS Styles panel. In this example, you'll edit a CSS style.

2   With the Alice Ritter text still selected, in the CSS Styles panel mouse over the font attribute. It says "This property is set in rule 'content h3' in file styles.css," as shown in the previous figure.

3   To find the file styles.css, click All in the CSS Styles panel.

4   Styles.css is the second top-level heading in the All panel, and if you expand it, you can see the names of all of the classes and IDs defined in the styles.css file.

5   Scroll down until you see ".content h3", and double-click it.

6   In the CSS Rule Definition dialog box, change the Text-transform property to lowercase, and then click Apply.

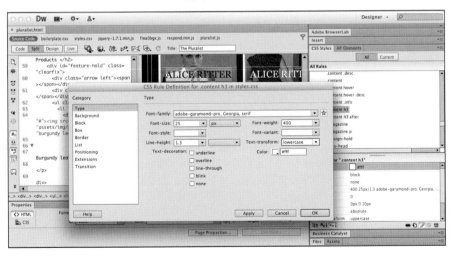

▶ **Tip:** If you only want to change the attributes of the selected element, you can use the Properties panel. To change all elements that use a CSS rule, edit attributes in the CSS Rule Definition dialog box.

Notice that more than one instance of the Alice Ritter text changes. The reason is that you are editing a CSS style, so any elements with that style applied will update.

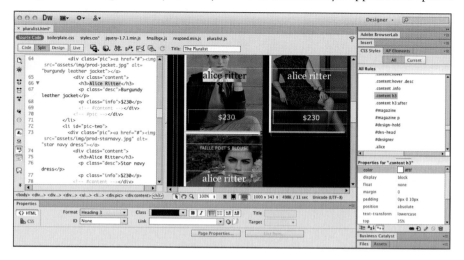

7 Click OK.

8 Click the File menu, and notice how the Save command is not available, but the Save All and Save All Related Files are available. Choose Save All Related Files.

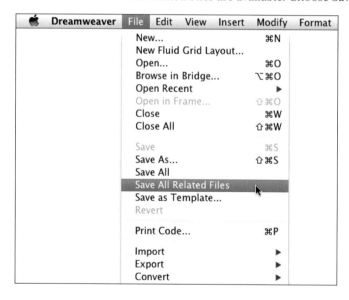

The Save command isn't available because you haven't actually changed the pluralist.html file. You changed the styles.css file that's linked from the pluralist.html file.

9 Close the pluralist.html file.

Inserting a Fireworks HTML page

Although Dreamweaver has powerful tools for laying out web pages, you may also want specialized tools for creating sophisticated website graphics, animations, and other assets. Adobe Fireworks possesses versatile tools for drawing and optimizing highly designed individual web pages, and Fireworks is tightly integrated with Dreamweaver. From the assets you export from a Fireworks document, you can pick and choose the elements you want to use: images, entire tables including sliced graphics, individual rollover buttons or ready-to-use navigation bars, or complete web pages with all elements already positioned.

You'll first export a mobile-sized page created in Fireworks CS6.

Exporting HTML pages from Fireworks

Fireworks can generate HTML pages and images directly from the Fireworks document—complete with functional navigation bar and rollover behaviors.

1   Start Fireworks.

2   Choose File > Open, and in the FW_png folder in the Lesson05 folder, locate the file fw_mobile.png. Select it and click Open.

If a warning about fonts appears, click Maintain Appearance. If you see any other warnings, simply click to accept them.

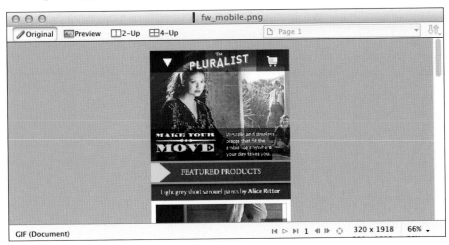

3   Choose File > Export.

4   In the Export dialog box, navigate to your Lesson05 folder.

5   Create a subfolder inside the Lesson05 folder: On Windows, right-click the file list pane and choose New > Folder. On Mac OS, click the New Folder button. Name the new folder **html_export**.

6 In the Export dialog box, you can leave the default name for the Save As option.

7 Choose HTML and Images from the Export menu. Choose Export HTML File from the HTML menu and Export Slices from the Slices menu. Choose All Pages from the Pages menu. Select the option Include Areas without Slices and make sure the Current State Only option is deselected.

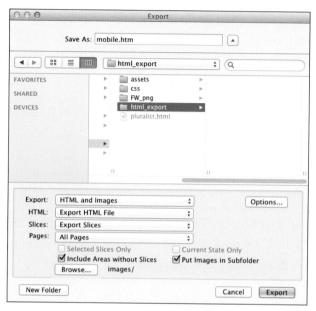

8 Select the option Put Images in Subfolder. By default, this will place all images in a folder named images inside the selected folder. Click Export.

9 When the export is complete, switch to Windows Explorer/the Finder. Navigate to the html_export subfolder inside the Lesson05 folder and double-click the file Page 1.htm. The page opens in your default web browser.

Including Fireworks Web Pages in Dreamweaver

The tight integration between Fireworks and Dreamweaver makes it very easy to create a Dreamweaver website from assets created in Fireworks. Simply export the elements you want to use from your Fireworks document, and then insert some or all of the elements into your Dreamweaver document.

Creating a new site

You'll begin by creating a new site in Dreamweaver. Part of the site creation process is to define a location on your hard drive where all the pages and images for your new website will be stored. This location is referred to as the local root folder for your Dreamweaver site.

1   In Dreamweaver CS6, choose New Site from the menu under the site icon at the top of the application frame.

2   In the Site Setup dialog box, type **Pluralist** for Site Name.

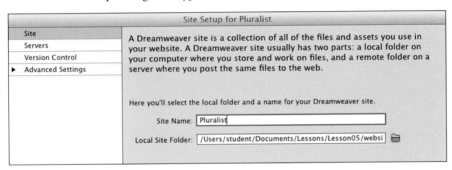

3   Click the Browse button beside Local Site Folder. Navigate to your Lesson05 folder, create a new folder called **Website** inside the Lesson05 folder, open it, and then click Select/Choose.

4   Click Save in the Site Setup dialog box.

5   Your new site is added to the Files panel where you can easily access and organize all the files that make up your website.

Creating new pages with CSS styles

Now you'll add blank HTML pages to your website into which you will place the HTML pages exported from Fireworks. The Dreamweaver pages will serve as containers for the Fireworks pages. The CSS style attached to the Dreamweaver pages will keep the placed images horizontally centered in the web browser window when the window is enlarged.

1 Choose File > New.

2 In the New Document dialog box, select the Blank Page category, if necessary, from the first column. In the Page Type column, select HTML. In the Layout column, select 1 column liquid, centered; then click Create.

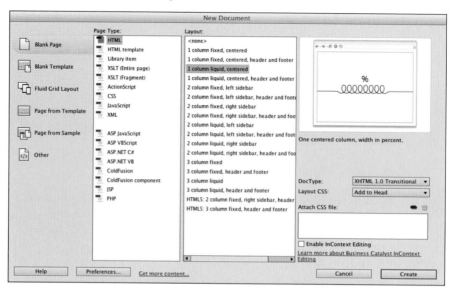

3 Choose File > Save As. In the Save As dialog box, click the Site Root button, type **home.html** in the File Name/Save As text box, and then click Save.

This simple web page layout has a CSS class named container assigned to a single div (page division) inside the body of the page. If this is starting to sound confusing, don't worry. We won't dive deep into the topic of CSS. For now, it's only important to understand that using CSS separates page content from page layout. For example, the style definition of the class container establishes that the content of the page (inside the container) remains horizontally centered on the page. You could easily change the content to be left aligned, for example, by editing the style definition. No change is necessary to the content of the page.

Inserting Fireworks HTML pages

You'll replace the entire content of the div container with the HTML page exported from Fireworks. You'll begin by setting the width of the container to the width of the HTML page it should contain.

1   Click anywhere in the dummy text of the home.htm page in Dreamweaver.

2   At the bottom of the document window, click the tag <div.container>, and then
    click the CSS Panel button in the Properties panel.

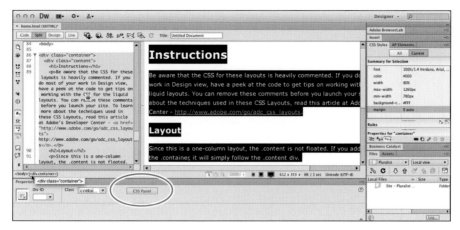

3   In the CSS Styles panel, click to the left of the max-width and min-width
    properties to disable them. For this mobile page design, you'll use a fixed width
    that matches the Fireworks document you're going to import.

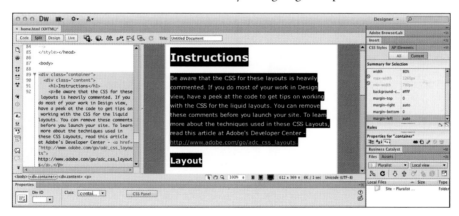

4 In the CSS Styles panel, double-click the Width property to open the CSS Rule Definition dialog box. Type **320** in the Width text box and choose px (pixels) from the units menu beside it. Click OK to close the dialog box.

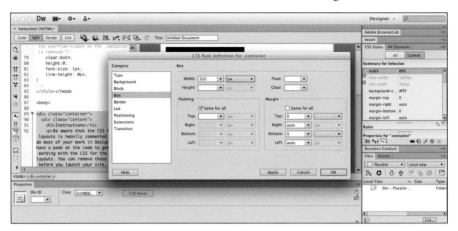

5 In Code view, select everything between the tags <div class="container"> and <!-- end .container --></div>, and then choose Insert > Image Objects > Fireworks HTML.

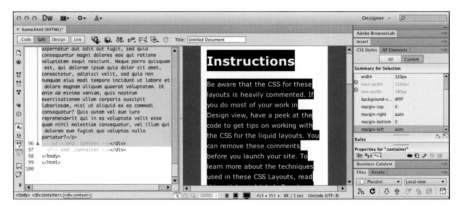

6 In the Insert Fireworks HTML dialog box, click the Browse button to locate the Fireworks HTML file you want to insert. In the Select the Fireworks HTML File dialog box, locate the html_export folder inside your Lesson05 folder, select the Page 1.htm file you exported earlier, and then click Open. Deselect the option Delete file after insertion, and then click OK to close the Insert Fireworks HTML dialog box.

7 In the warning dialog box, click OK to copy referenced files into the site folder.

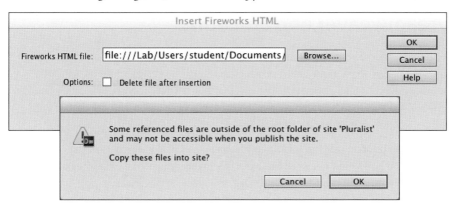

8 In the Copy Image Files To dialog box, navigate to the local root folder website, create a new folder inside that folder and name it **Images**, make sure the current folder is the new Images folder, and then click Select/Open.

9 In the document window, click the Refresh button to view your updated content.

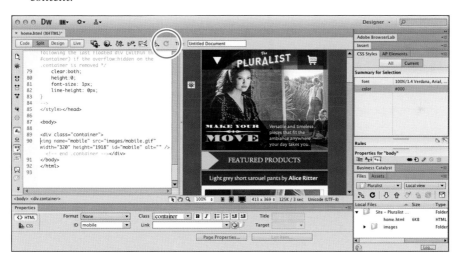

10 Choose File > Save and then choose File > Preview In Browser > *[Web Browser Name]*. The page opens in your default web browser. Enlarge the width of the browser window and notice that the image stays centered within the browser window, thanks to the HTML template you chose when you created the site.

11 Close the browser window and return to Dreamweaver.

Roundtrip Editing between Dreamweaver and Fireworks

When you need to edit the web page you imported from Fireworks, you can take advantage of the tight cross-product integration between Fireworks and Dreamweaver: In Fireworks, edit the original file in PNG format, which was used to generate the Fireworks HTML pages, and the changes will be incorporated automatically when you return to Dreamweaver.

To enable roundtrip editing for the main image in GIF file format on the home page you created, Fireworks needs to be set as the primary external editor for GIF images in Dreamweaver. This can be done in Dreamweaver Preferences.

Setting Fireworks as primary editor for GIF images

You can set Fireworks as the primary editor for GIF images on your system. Thereafter, opening GIFs in Windows Explorer or the Mac Finder will launch Fireworks.

1   Choose Edit > Preferences/Dreamweaver > Preferences.

2   Select File Types/Editors from the Category list.

3   Select .gif from the Extensions list.

4   Select Fireworks from the Editors list, and then click the Make Primary button.

5   With Fireworks set as primary editor for .gif images, click OK to close the Preferences dialog box.

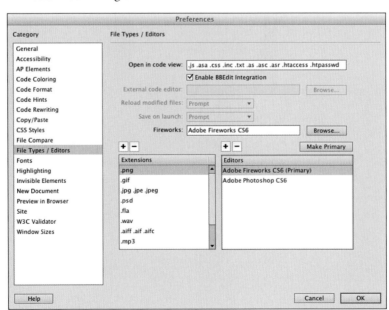

Edit the original Fireworks PNG file of a GIF image placed in Dreamweaver

Changes made to a source PNG file in Fireworks can flow automatically into Dreamweaver. Here we'll update a GIF image in Dreamweaver by editing the original Fireworks PNG from which it was created.

1 In Design view, right-click/Control-click anywhere in the main image in the Design view in Dreamweaver and choose Edit With > Adobe Fireworks CS6.

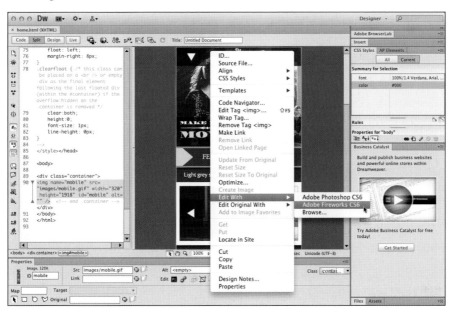

2 In the Find Source for Editing dialog box, click the Use a PNG button.

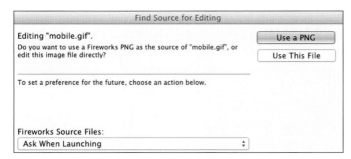

3 In the Open/Open File dialog box, navigate to the Lesson05 folder, select the file fw_mobile.png, and then click Open. If a warning about fonts appears, click Maintain Appearance.

4   Fireworks opens the PNG file in a special editing window, which is indicated by an additional bar across the top of the window. If you see an alert about the structure of the HTML table, click OK.

5   Select the brown rectangle behind the text FEATURED PRODUCTS, click the fill swatch in the Color Palette panel, and choose black.

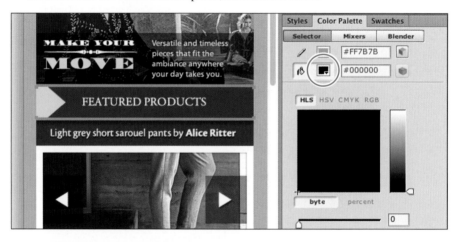

6 Click Done in the bar across the top of the editing window. This will save your edits, close the file, and return to Dreamweaver.

In Dreamweaver, the GIF image used for the home page in Dreamweaver is automatically updated to reflect the color change you made to the PNG document.

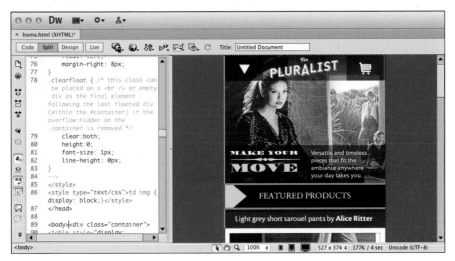

7 Close the home.html file; if you're asked to save changes, click Save.

Wrapping Up

Congratulations; you've completed this brief introduction to Dreamweaver and Fireworks! You learned how to use Dreamweaver to design a website that responds dynamically to a wide range of screen sizes, how to inspect and edit CSS elements on a web page, and how to create a roundtrip editing workflow between Fireworks and Dreamweaver.

Review questions

1 What is the reason for the name of the Dreamweaver feature fluid grid layout?

2 What does the Live button do in Dreamweaver?

3 How can you preview a web page design on multiple display sizes at once in Dreamweaver?

4 Why would you want to design some parts of a website in Fireworks and the rest of the site in Dreamweaver?

5 Explain roundtrip editing between Dreamweaver and Fireworks.

Review answers

1 A fluid grid layout is responsive in that it can automatically adapt to different screen sizes, such as desktop, tablet, and mobile displays.

2 Clicking the Live button enables Live view, which renders a web page in Dreamweaver as it would appear in a WebKit-based browser so that you see a more accurate preview.

3 You can preview a web page design at three sizes simultaneously by using Multiscreen Preview, which you can customize.

4 Fireworks and Dreamweaver complement each other. Dreamweaver excels at the structural layout and organization of an overall website. Fireworks specializes in high-quality graphics and interactivity.

5 An image that was exported from Fireworks and then placed in Dreamweaver can be edited by opening the PNG file from which the image was created in Fireworks, making the adjustments, and then reexporting and placing the image in Dreamweaver. This process is automated if you follow these steps:

- To set Fireworks as the primary image editor for the relevant image format, choose Edit With > Fireworks from within Dreamweaver.

- Select the original PNG when prompted.

- Edit the image in Fireworks.

6 CREATING INTERACTIVE FORMS

Lesson Overview

In this lesson you'll learn how to create PDF forms by using new form tools in Adobe InDesign. You'll learn these skills and techniques:

- Quickly laying out a form using a table grid

- Adding different types of form objects, such as text fields, radio buttons, check boxes, and combo boxes

- Duplicating form objects

- Testing your form in Adobe Acrobat X Pro

 You'll probably need about an hour to complete this lesson.

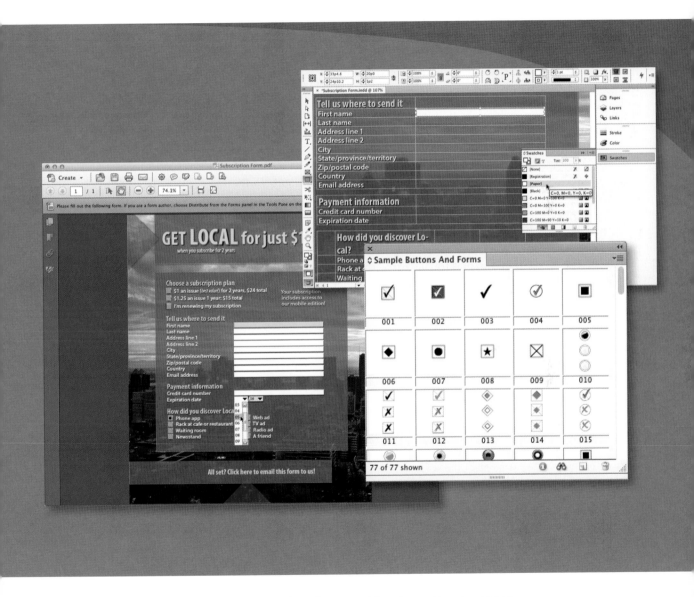

Learn how to combine advanced layout and typography tools with powerful new form tools in Adobe InDesign CS6 to produce PDF forms that are easy to fill out.

Creating PDF Forms in Adobe InDesign

Adobe InDesign CS6 includes form-building tools that you can use together with its advanced layout and typography features to create PDF forms that are functional and well designed. The forms tools in InDesign CS6 are a step up from those in InDesign CS5. You could design a form in InDesign CS5, but converting design elements to a functional form was done in Adobe Acrobat X Pro. Now you can accomplish most form-building tasks in InDesign CS6 alone, although you'll still check your work in Acrobat X Pro.

The decisions you make with the form tools should be based on the data formats required for your data to be processed correctly by the database that will receive it. Before you begin designing an interactive form, discuss your goals with your web developers and have them review the design, the form field values, and any code or scripts used in the form. They might suggest ways to set up your form so that it collects your data efficiently and integrates smoothly with the receiving database.

Getting Started

The form that you'll work with in this lesson is already partially built. It's saved as a template file in your Lesson06 folder. You'll open it and take a look at how it's been put together so far.

1 In Adobe Bridge, navigate to the Lesson06 folder in your Lessons folder.

2 Double-click the file Subscription Form.indt to open it in InDesign CS6.

3 Choose View > Fit Page in Window.

The partially built form is in the large rectangle in the middle of the page. The form structure may not be visible if the document opened in the Preview screen mode.

4 Choose File > Save As, enter the filename **Subscription Form.indd**, navigate to your Lesson06 folder, and click Save.

5 Choose View > Screen Mode and make sure Normal is selected, or press the W key to toggle the screen mode to Normal. In Normal screen mode, the text frames and table grid are visible. Although you can edit in Preview mode, you'll probably find it easier to work in Normal mode where object outlines are visible.

6 Zoom in so that you can see the top of the form more clearly.

To make it easy to align form objects with their labels, this form is laid out using a table. You'll paste form objects into it as inline graphics so they flow with the table. You can also lay out forms using text with tabs or even as individual text and form objects that you select and line up using the Align panel. For the form used in this lesson, it was decided that a table would be the simplest way to develop this form.

Preview screen mode

Normal screen mode

Using the Sample Buttons and Forms Panel

Next, you'll add radio buttons and check boxes to the form.

1   Choose Window > Interactive > Buttons and Forms.

You use this panel to control how a form object works, but the options in the panel are available only when a form object is selected. There aren't any form objects in this document yet, only the layout and text for the form, so you'll add some form objects now. Fortunately, instead of having to design them from scratch, you can use premade form objects.

2   Choose Sample Buttons And Forms from the Button and Forms panel menu, and then scroll the panel to examine the form objects that are available.

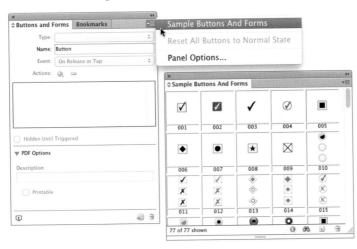

The Sample Buttons and Forms panel is an InDesign library containing a range of check boxes, radio buttons, and buttons of various shapes and designs.

3 In the Sample Buttons and Forms panel, drag the radio button set 017 to the left of the heading for the first group of options, "Choose a subscription plan." The exact position doesn't matter right now.

Note: When a form object, such as a button, radio button, or check box, is selected on the layout, you may see multiple states listed in the Buttons and Forms panel. These provide the alternate appearances of a form object that indicate when it's selected or not selected, or when the mouse pointer is over it.

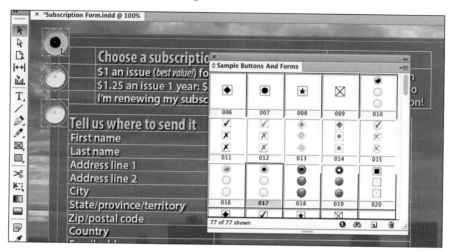

4 With the three radio buttons still selected, make sure the "Constrain proportions for width & height" button is selected in the Control panel, enter **1p2** into the W (Width) field in the Control panel, and press Enter/Return.

Note: There are two different Constrain Proportions (link) icons near each other in the Control panel, so make sure you click the correct one as shown in the figure for step 4.

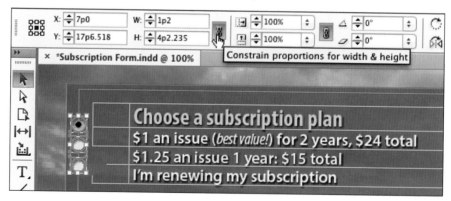

5 Choose Edit > Deselect All.

6 With the Selection tool (▸), select the first radio button and choose Edit > Cut.

7 With the Type tool (T,), click an insertion point in the table cell to the left of the label "$1 an issue..." and choose Edit > Paste.

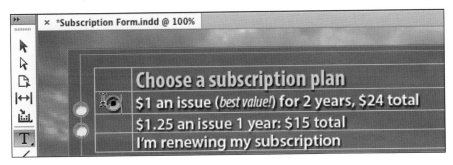

8 Repeat step 6 for the second radio button, pasting it into the table cell below the first radio button.

The third choice, "I'm renewing my subscription," is actually independent of the first two. You'll replace it with a check box so that the person filling out the form can first select a subscription plan and then specify whether it is a renewal.

9 With the Selection tool, select the third radio button and press the Delete key.

10 In the Sample Buttons and Forms panel, drag the check box 001 to the left of the two radio buttons; again, the exact placement isn't critical.

11 With the check box still selected, make sure the "Constrain proportions for width & height" button is selected in the Control panel, enter **1p2** into the W (Width) field in the Control panel, and press Enter/Return.

12 With the Selection tool, select the check box and choose Edit > Cut.

13 With the Type tool, click an insertion point in the table cell to the left of the label "I'm renewing..." and choose Edit > Paste.

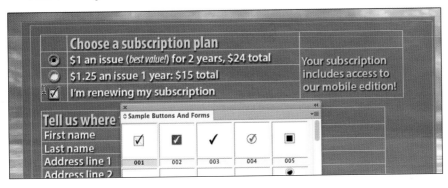

14 Choose Edit > Deselect All, and save the document.

Checking Your Work So Far

You can't preview form interactions in InDesign CS6, so you'll do a quick export to Adobe Acrobat X Pro to make sure the form is working properly so far.

1 Choose File > Export.

2 For the format, choose Adobe PDF (Interactive), and click Save.

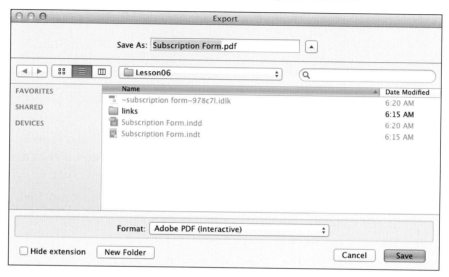

3 In the Export to Interactive PDF dialog box, make sure View After Exporting is selected, and make sure Include All is selected in the Forms and Media section.

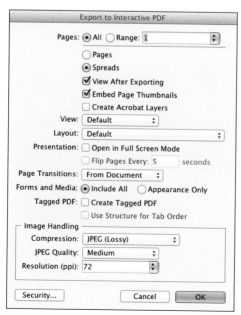

4 Leave the other settings at the default and click OK.

When the document opens in Acrobat, the form objects you added may look a little different because Acrobat highlights form objects.

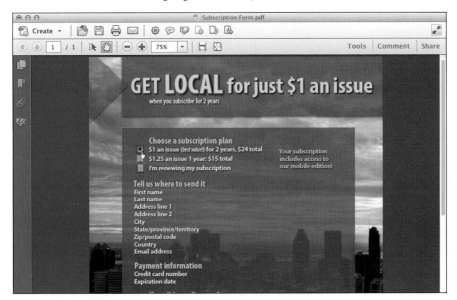

5 Click the radio buttons and the check box you added to make sure they work. Only one of the radio buttons should be selected at any time, and you should be able to click to toggle the check box on and off.

6 When you're done, close the PDF file without saving changes, and switch back to InDesign.

If you leave the PDF file open, it may prevent InDesign from replacing it when you later export an updated PDF file.

● **Note:** Old or non-Adobe PDF readers may not support form features. For best results, preview forms in the most recent version of Acrobat Pro or Adobe Reader.

Adding Text Fields

Adding text entry fields into an InDesign form is as easy as drawing a rectangle, because you can convert a selected rectangle to a text field. You'll do this to build most of the two middle sections of the form. Fortunately, you can duplicate text fields, which will save you work.

1   With the Rectangle tool (▭), draw a rectangle that roughly fits in the table cell to the right of the First Name label. You'll fine-tune the size next.

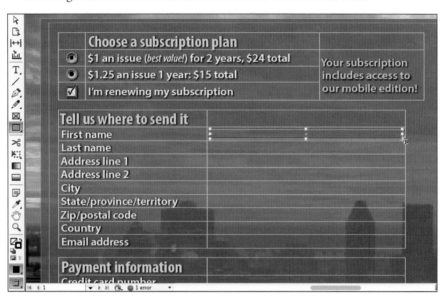

● **Note:** Although you can convert any closed shape to a text field, in Acrobat it will always appear as a rectangle.

2   With the rectangle selected, in the Control panel deselect the "Constrain proportions for width & height" button, enter **20p** into the W (Width) field, enter **1p2** into the H (Height) field, and press Enter/Return.

3   In the Swatches panel, set the fill color to Paper and the stroke color to None.

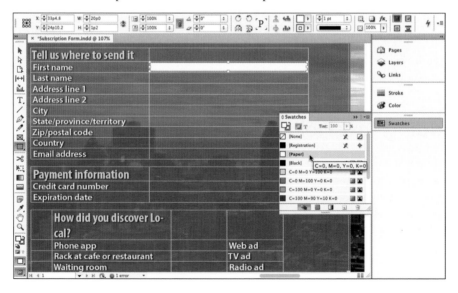

In this way you can customize the appearance of a rectangular text field. Given the colored background of this form design, a white fill color helps keep the text fields legible, even if the form is printed and filled out by hand.

4   With the rectangle selected, in the Buttons and Forms panel choose Text Field from the Type menu.

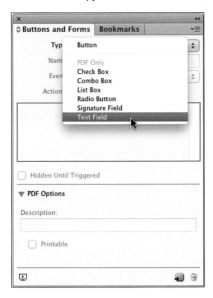

5   Near the bottom of the Buttons and Forms panel, select the Required check box in the PDF Options group.

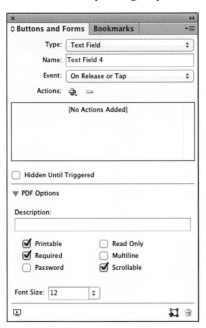

If some form fields are not optional, you can mark them as Required. This will outline them in red in the exported PDF file when Highlight Existing Fields is on.

6 With the Selection tool, select the rectangle and choose Edit > Cut.

7 With the Type tool, click an insertion point in the table cell to the right of the First Name label and choose Edit > Paste.

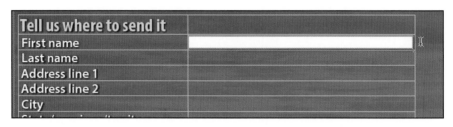

● **Note:** If the export fails because you get a warning about permission issues or the file being in use, first make sure the previous PDF draft isn't still open in Acrobat. If that doesn't work, try quitting Acrobat, and also try deleting the previous PDF draft.

8 Save the document and repeat steps 1–4 in the section "Checking Your Work So Far" to export another draft of the PDF form. If you get a warning that "Subscription Form.pdf" already exists, click the Replace button.

9 In Acrobat, type a name into the First Name field you created.

The field should work fine, but the text may be slightly large for the field. In the figure below, the descenders of some letters are cut off. Before you create the rest of the text fields, you'll resolve this issue.

10 Close the PDF file without saving changes, and return to InDesign.

11 With the Selection tool, select the rectangle, and in the Buttons and Forms panel choose Auto from the Font Size menu.

The Auto option resizes text so that it's always completely visible inside a text field. However, if a large amount of text is entered into a small field, the text may become very small. With the short bits of text that will be entered into these fields, that should not be a problem.

Now you'll finish off the rest of the text fields.

12 With the Selection tool, select the rectangle and choose Edit > Copy.

13 With the Type tool, click an insertion point in the table cell to the right of the Last Name label and choose Edit > Paste.

▶ **Tip:** You can still change attributes of each text field after pasting the duplicate text fields. For example, if you don't want the form to require "Address line 2" because not all addresses have a second address line, select the field after "Address line 2" and deselect the Required check box in the Buttons and Forms panel.

▶ **Tip:** In form fields that are large enough, an icon in the bottom right corner indicates the field type.

14 Repeat step 13 for the subsequent table cells, pasting the last text field to the right of the Expiration Date label.

Using appropriate form objects

Each choice you have for form objects has a specific purpose, so it's best to choose the appropriate type. Here's how to pick the right form object for the job:

- A button is best used to initiate an action, such as playing a video or submitting a form.

- A check box group represents options that aren't mutually exclusive—you can pick more than one. For example, you could use check boxes to let users indicate which countries they have visited.

- A radio button represents options that are mutually exclusive—you can pick only one. For example, you could use radio buttons to let someone indicate the country in which they were born. You wouldn't want to use check boxes for this purpose because it would allow users to select multiple countries of birth, which would be invalid.

- A list box presents a scrolling list of options. You can allow multiple selections in a list box.

- A combo box presets a drop-down menu of items from which you can select only one. Also, a combo box allows direct text entry.

- A signature field lets someone enter a digital signature using a stylus or tablet.

- A text field allows entry of text.

If a form object has options, you'll find them in the Buttons and Forms panel when the object is selected.

Creating Combo Boxes

Now you'll use combo boxes to simplify the entry of the credit card expiration date. You'll use the pasted rectangle as a starting point.

1   With the Selection tool, select the rectangle you pasted to the right of the Expiration Date label.

2   In the Control panel, enter **3p** into the W (width) field, and press Enter/Return.

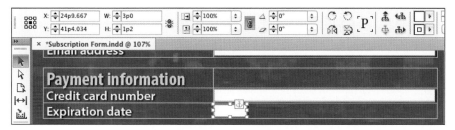

3   With the rectangle still selected, in the Buttons and Forms panel choose Combo Box from the Type menu.

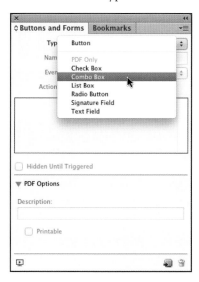

Now you'll create a list of months from 01 to 12.

4   Enter **01** in the List Items option that appears at the bottom of the Buttons and Forms panel, and press the + button or Enter/Return. Repeat for **02**, **03**, and so on until you get to **12**.

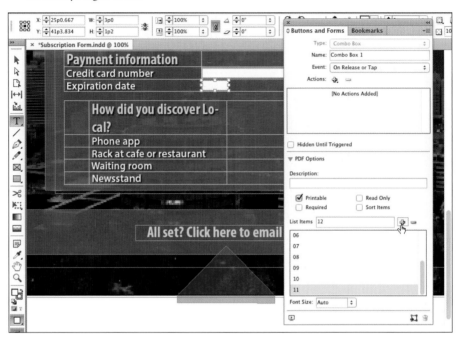

Tip: You can change the order of a form object's list by dragging the items up or down.

5   With the Type tool, click to the right of the month combo box you just created and type a slash character (/). This is the slash that typically appears between the month and year.

6   With the Selection tool, select the month combo box and choose Edit > Copy.

7   With the Type tool, click an insertion point in the table cell to the right of the slash and choose Edit > Paste.

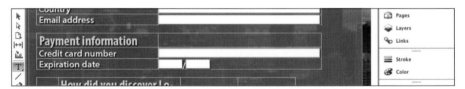

Next you'll create a list of the next few years.

8   With the Selection tool, click the rectangle you just pasted and select the 01 list item in the Buttons and Forms panel and click the – (minus) button to remove it from the list. Repeat until only the one "12" item remains.

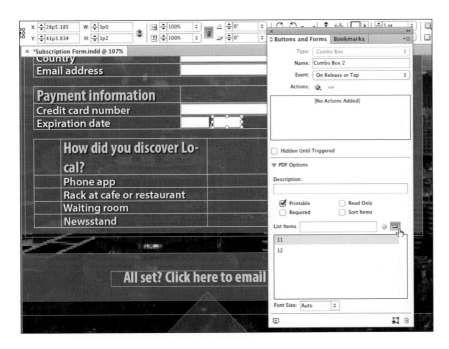

9 As you did in step 4, create a list, but this time have the series go from **2012** to **2018**.

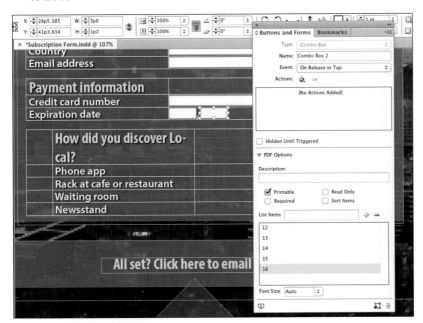

10 Save the document and export another version to PDF.

11 In Acrobat, try out the text fields and the combo boxes you just made.

12 Because this is just a test, close the PDF document without saving changes. Then return to InDesign.

Finishing the Form Objects

The table holding the form elements could use some tidying up. But first you'll finish the set of radio buttons at the bottom of the form, as well as the submission button.

1 With the Type tool, highlight the radio button next to "$1 an issue…" at the top of the form, and choose Edit > Copy.

2 With the Type tool, click an insertion point in the table cell next to the Phone App label near the bottom of the form, and choose Edit > Paste.

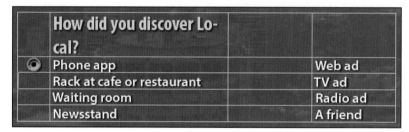

3 With the Selection tool, select the radio button you just pasted, and in the Buttons and Forms panel, change the name to **Discovery**.

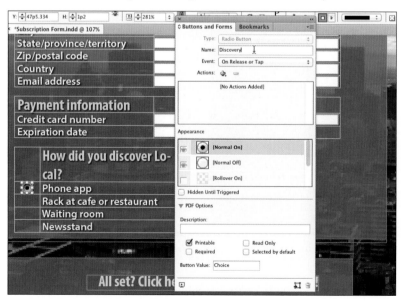

Changing the name is necessary because you're starting a different group of radio buttons. If all radio buttons on a page had the same name, selecting one radio button would deselect all other radio buttons on the page.

4 With the Type tool, highlight the radio button you just renamed, and copy and paste it into the other seven cells at the bottom of the form as shown.

The last item to make interactive is the text field at the very bottom of the page.

5 With the Selection tool, select the text frame containing the text "All set? Click here to email…"

6 In the Buttons and Forms panel, choose Button from the Type menu.

7 In the Buttons and Forms panel, click the plus sign menu next to the Actions label and choose Submit Form.

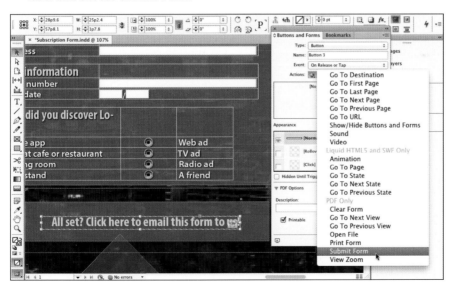

Normally, the next step would be to enter a path in the URL field, which would lead to a web server that is set up to receive the data in this form, but for this lesson you'll omit that step.

8 Save the document and export another version to PDF.

9 In Acrobat, try out the text fields and the combo boxes you just made.

10 Because this is just a test, close the PDF document without saving changes. Then return to InDesign.

Cleaning Up the Table Containing the Form

You've probably noticed that the table headings aren't all aligned. You'll tidy up the table before you export the final version.

1 With the Type tool, drag to select the first two cells at the top of the form as shown in the following figure, and choose Table > Merge Cells.

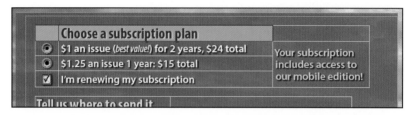

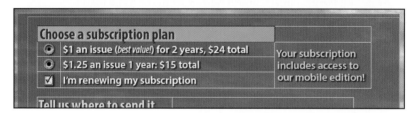

2 Drag the Type tool down the three cells containing the radio buttons and the check box, and in the Control panel, click the Align Left button.

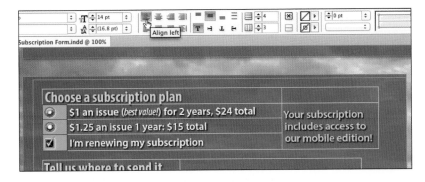

3   Position the pointer over the vertical cell border next to the three cells you just aligned, and drag to the left to remove the extra space.

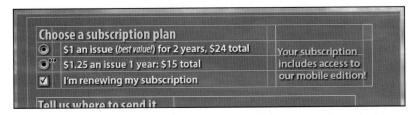

4   Select the first two cells in the table containing the "How did you discover Local?" radio button group, and choose Table > Merge Cells.

5   Align the radio buttons and adjust the vertical cell borders until they are more consistent, similar to step 3 and as shown in the following figure.

Now the headings are all aligned and are no longer too long for their cells.

6 Save the document and export another version to PDF.

Tip: If you're distracted by Acrobat form field highlighting, click to deselect the Highlight Existing Fields button in the purple form toolbar at the top of the Acrobat window.

7 In Acrobat, try out the text fields and the combo boxes you just made. When you click the "All set? Click here…" link you set up at the bottom of the form, it will produce a warning; click Cancel. It is currently not set up to do anything, but in a real form it would be set up to submit the form data to an actual web server.

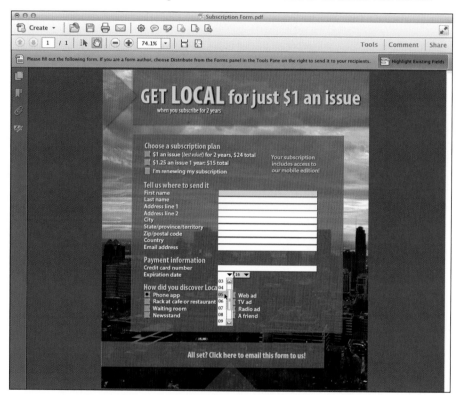

Tip: To let users of Adobe Reader 8 and later save data they enter into your PDF form, open it in Acrobat X Pro and choose File > Save As > Reader Extended PDF > Enable Additional Features. Click Save Now in the dialog box that appears, and then save it under a new name.

8 Close the PDF document without saving changes, and return to InDesign.

9 Close the InDesign document, and if you're asked if you want to save changes, click Save.

Throughout this lesson you haven't been saving changes to the PDF document, because you've only been testing the form. Saving changes to a PDF form is necessary when you're entering data that you want to keep; a form recipient would want to save the changes.

Review questions

1 Why is it important to consult with your web developer before designing a form?

2 What's the main difference between radio buttons and check boxes?

3 Why do some of the sample form objects have three versions?

4 If selecting a radio button deselects all other radio buttons in other button groups instead of only within the same group, how do you fix it?

5 If a recipient is not able to fill out a PDF form, what will probably resolve the issue?

Review answers

1 When a form is submitted electronically, the form field data must be formatted properly for the database that will receive it.

2 You can make only one selection from a group of radio buttons, but you can make multiple selections from a group of check boxes.

3 Form objects can support multiple visual states, so that the object can look different depending on whether it's on or off, or the pointer is over it.

4 All buttons within a radio button group must use the same name, but the button name of each group must be different. If buttons are switching on and off in other groups, some buttons may be using a name of another button group.

5 Make sure the recipient is using a recent version of Acrobat Pro or Adobe Reader, because older versions or non-Adobe software that reads PDF files may not fully support form features.

7 SUBMITTING WORK FOR A PDF REVIEW

Lesson Overview

In this lesson you'll be introduced to the different types of PDF review and learn the techniques you'll need to take advantage of the exciting collaborative features in Acrobat and CS6:

- Attaching a PDF for an e-mail-based review

- Adding and replying to comments

- Customizing the appearance of your notes

- Marking up a document

- Collaborating in online meetings

- Initiating a server-based shared review

- Tracking and managing PDF reviews

- Protecting your work

- Hosting a real-time online web conference

 You'll probably need between one and two hours to complete this lesson.

Whether you want to get input on a spreadsheet or to collaborate on a design project, or you just need a project approved, Acrobat facilitates a range of review workflows. You can set up a review to suit your needs and have Acrobat keep track of comments, send notifications, and more. You can also collaborate live in online meetings—all in secure settings.

Introducing the Different Types of Review

Note: Before you start working on this lesson, make sure that you've installed the Creative Suite 6 Design & Web Premium software on your computer, and that you have correctly copied the Lessons folder from the disc in the back of this book onto your computer's hard drive (see "Copying the Classroom in a Book files" on page 2).

When it's time to present and share your work, Acrobat delivers many features to facilitate the review process. You have a choice between different types of review—and for each there's a wizard to guide you step by step through the process.

The e-mail-based review

An e-mail-based review is an excellent option when reviewers do not have access to a remote server or when it's unnecessary to interact with each other directly or in real time. Reviewers in an e-mail-based review have the opportunity to interact by replying to each other's comments once the initiator of the review has merged them. Later in this lesson you'll add and reply to comments in an e-mail-based review.

Note: Only users of Acrobat X Pro can initiate a document review and invite users of Adobe Reader to participate.

To start this review, the initiator sends an e-mail invitation to review the PDF file by clicking Send for Email Review, which is in the Review panel in the Comment pane. The e-mailed PDF file includes comment and markup tools for the addressees to state their opinions. The Tracker enables the initiator to automatically merge those reviewers' comments into the master copy when monitoring them. You'll be guided through this process later in this lesson.

The shared review

The highly collaborative nature of the shared review makes it the perfect solution for a group of people with common access to a centralized server. A shared review allows reviewers to read and reply to the comments of other participants rather than only being able to do so through the initiator.

When you initiate a shared review, you post a PDF file by clicking Send for Shared Review, which is in the Review panel in the Comment pane. The review can be hosted online in two ways: on Acrobat.com or by specifying your own server location (a network folder, a Windows server running Microsoft SharePoint Services, or a web server folder). The reviewers receive an e-mail message with a link to the review location online. When they click the link, they can review the document in their web browser (if the PDF plug-in is installed) or they can download the PDF file and review the document within Acrobat of the free Acrobat Reader. Reviewers can see the comments that other reviewers have made.

The Tracker in Acrobat facilitates the entire review process: Not only will the comments be merged and collected, but you can also invite additional reviewers as well as send e-mail reminders to participants.

The online, real-time review

There's no better way to show and tell than sharing your work online and live via your desktop. If you have an account on Acrobat.com, you can conduct real-time meetings on your desktop using Adobe ConnectNow, a personal web-conference tool. You can share individual applications or your entire screen to others attending the online meeting through their web browsers, and you can upload and share most document types. These options are especially useful when you want to share files in formats other than PDF or when you want to demonstrate an action within an application. A real-time online review can save much time in collaborative discussions—not to mention reduced travel costs! You can start a real-time review and a ConnectNow screen sharing from Acrobat X Pro.

Participants join the meeting by logging in to a web-based meeting space from their own computers. In addition to sharing a document or your entire desktop, in a ConnectNow online meeting you can use live chat, share online whiteboards, and take advantage of many other collaborative features.

Collaborating in an e-mail-based review

For the purposes of this lesson, in which you'll be exchanging comments regarding the magazine cover you designed in Lesson 2, the process of conducting the review will be simplified. You may not have access to a shared server or a partner to participate in the review, but you can still get to know the relevant features in Acrobat and the interface and tools you'll use to collaborate in a review.

Following are the steps of this hypothetical review:

1   You initiate the review by using Acrobat to open a PDF file from your Lessons folder and using an e-mail-based review to send the PDF file to your selected reviewers as an e-mail attachment.

2   You can review this PDF attachment, adding your remarks using the comment and markup tools in Acrobat or the free Adobe Reader.

3   Use the Tracker to monitor the comments that each reviewer has added to the PDF file.

Viewing comments

Your task is to review a magazine cover—in this case not sent as an e-mail attachment but as a PDF file in your Lessons folder—and add your comments using the comment tools in Acrobat. You'll first want to view and assess the comments of other reviewers.

1   If you haven't already done so, launch Adobe Bridge.

2   In Adobe Bridge, navigate to your Lesson07 folder and double-click the file Local_Magazine_start_cover.pdf to open it in Acrobat X Pro.

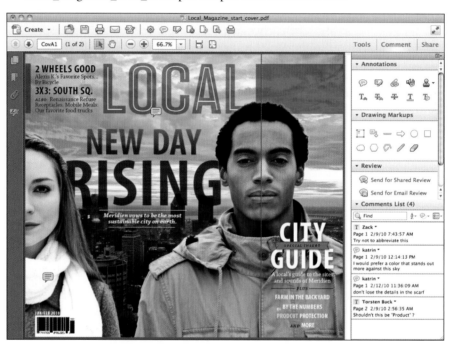

Note: In Reader, the complete set of comment tools are available only for PDF files in which commenting is enabled. PDF files in a review workflow typically include commenting rights.

3   If the Comment pane is not already open, click Comments on the right side of the Acrobat workspace. The Comment pane contains four panels:

- **Annotations** lets you or a reviewer mark up a PDF file with comments by highlighting, adding sticky notes, making text corrections, and more.

- **Drawing Markups** lets you or a reviewer add comments using shapes, lines, arrows, and more, such as when you want to circle an area of a page.

- **Review** provides the review options described in this section, and lets you manage them with the Tracker (see "Working with the Tracker" later in this lesson.

- **Comments List** shows you all of the comments saved with the PDF file. You can check off or set the status of comments as you address them, and you can reply to comments. The Comments List is also a great way to make sure you see all comments, because small annotations can be easy to miss on a page.

4 If you don't see a list of comments, click Comments List at the bottom of the Comment pane.

By default, comments are sorted according to the page on which they appear. However, you can change that order to sort the comments by author, type, date, or checked status.

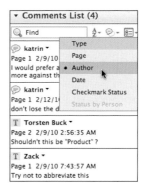

5 Change the sorting order by clicking Sort Comments in the Comments List and choosing Date.

6 Click the yellow sticky note under the name Katrin. Acrobat will highlight the corresponding sticky note on the document with a blue halo.

7 Move the pointer over the highlighted yellow sticky note on the magazine cover. A tool tip pops up to display the comment text.

▶ **Tip:** To view only the comments of a particular reviewer, click the Filter button on the Comments List toolbar, choose Reviewer, and then select the name of the reviewer. All comments from other reviewers will be hidden. To display all of the comments, choose Show Reviewer > All.

8 Double-click the yellow sticky note icon to open the associated pop-up window, and then drag to position the pop-up window anywhere you want on the magazine cover.

Sending a file for an e-mail-based review

For an e-mail-based review, you can send out a tracked copy of a PDF, which makes it easy to collect and manage all the responses. You can explore this option provided you have an Internet connection, an e-mail address, and a colleague to work with.

1   In Acrobat, open the PDF file you want to send for review.

2   On the right side of the Acrobat workspace, click Comment to open the Comment pane, if necessary. In the Review panel, choose Send for Email Review. If this is the first time you've used this feature, the Identity Setup dialog box appears. You'll need to enter your information before proceeding.

3   The Attach for Email Review command opens a wizard to guide you through the process of attaching a PDF file and specifying a master copy. All comments from the reviewers will be merged into this file.

4   Enter the e-mail addresses of the reviewers. To enter addresses faster, click Address Book to select addresses from the address book of the default e-mail application on your system.

5   Click Next. You can preview and edit the Subject and the Message of the e-mail that will be sent to the recipients.

6   Click Send Invitation. A copy of the PDF is sent to the reviewers as an attachment. It may be opened in your e-mail program, and you may need to send it manually from there.

When this PDF attachment is opened, it displays comment tools and instructions.

Whenever you receive comments to the review you initiated, the Merge Comments dialog box will appear. You can then merge the comments into the master PDF so that they're all in one location.

All comments can be moved around the page except text markups. You'll appreciate this when you receive documents for review that are cluttered with comments.

You can hide or show comments by filtering them based on the reviewer. When you summarize or print comments, you can specify whether hidden comments appear. Hiding a comment that has been replied to will hide the entire thread associated with that comment—that is, all the replies and discussion on the comment.

● **Note:** In an e-mail-based review, hidden comments aren't included when you send your comments to the initiator.

Replying to a comment

When you've seen the other comments and are part of the review, you'll probably want to put in your two cents' worth as well. Acrobat gives you a wide choice of comment and markup tools for providing feedback and communicating your ideas.

Not only can you type text comments into the familiar sticky notes, you can also add arrows and shapes, and draw freehand directly onto the file to illustrate your point or highlight parts of the text and add callouts. You can modify the appearance of your comments by changing the color of the sticky notes or the type style, which you'll be doing as part of the next exercise. An array of stamps helps you to efficiently comment and mark standard business documents, and you can also create and customize your own stamps. Provided you have the appropriate hardware and software installed, Acrobat even lets you add audio comments.

Next, you'll reply to one of those yellow sticky notes from this e-mail-based review.

1 With the Comments List still open, select the comment from Katrin that says, "don't lose the details in the scarf."

Uploading a file for a live collaborative review

By using the Acrobat.com online service, you can communicate via live chat and review a PDF file live online with your colleagues.

1   In Acrobat, open the PDF file you want to send for review.

2   On the right side of the Acrobat workspace, click the Comment pane, and then click Review.

3   Click Collaborate Live.

4   Sign in to Acrobat.com with your Adobe ID (or click Create Adobe ID to make one), and then click Next.

5   Preview and edit the recipients, Subject, and Message of the e-mail that will be sent to reviewers. Clicking the To and CC buttons lets you select addresses from the address book of the default e-mail application on your system.

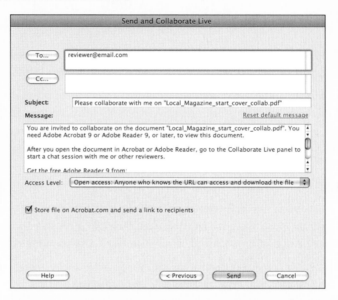

6   Select the Store File on Acrobat.com and Send a Link to Recipients check box to host your PDF file on Acrobat.com. This is useful when the PDF file is large because the e-mail doesn't need to include an attachment; instead, the recipient gets just an e-mail and a download link. If you prefer to send an attachment, leave the Store File on Acrobat.com and Send a Link to Recipients check box deselected.

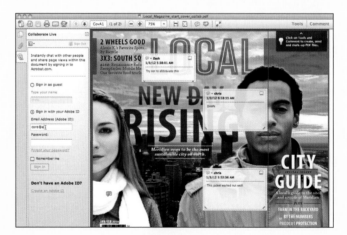

7   Click Send. When the PDF file is opened by you or any recipient, it displays the Review panel, which provides the opportunity to go online and start a live collaborative review immediately.

2 Click the black triangle next to Katrin's name at the top of her comment, and in the menu that appears, choose Set Status > Rejected. The black triangle next to the reviewer's name reminds you that an Options menu is available.

The rejected status is indicated by a red cross next to your name, because you're the one who set that status.

3 In the same comment, click the black triangle next to Katrin's name and choose Reply, the first command in the menu.

4 The comment extends with an indented area labeled with your name where you can explain in your reply why you rejected the design, such as: **We checked the numbers and it also proofs properly. Thanks**.

5 If the sticky note's comment window is open on the page, you can reply the same way you did in the Comments List—by clicking the black triangle next to Katrin's name to choose Reply from the menu that appears.

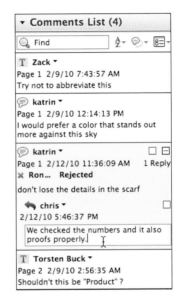

6 Close the sticky note by clicking the Close button on the top-right side of the sticky note.

Customizing the appearance of your notes

Finally, you'll add your own comment using the Annotations panel, and then change the color of the sticky note to make your statement more prominent.

1 In the top toolbar, select the Sticky Note tool ( ). Click to add a new sticky note on the man's shoulder.

2 If the yellow sticky note isn't open, double-click to open it, and then type your comment. We wrote: **This jacket worked out well!**

Note: To delete a comment, right-click / Control-click the sticky note and choose Delete.

3 Click the black triangle next to your name on the note to open the Options menu, and choose Properties.

▶ **Tip:** If you want a Properties dialog box change to apply to future comments, turn on the Make Properties Default check box at the bottom of the Properties dialog box.

4 In the Sticky Note Properties dialog box, click the Color swatch to open the color picker, choose a bright blue, and then click OK.

5 Now your note stands out among the others.

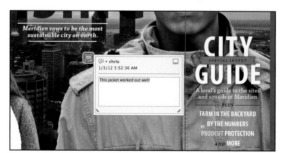

Marking up a document

Although you now know how to add a comment using the Sticky Note tool from the top toolbar, there are many more tools in the Annotations panel of the Comment pane. You can use text edit tools to indicate where to insert or replace text, or underline text. You can also cross out text to mark it for deletion. Your text edit comments do not alter the content of the PDF file; they merely indicate where text should be inserted and which text should be deleted or replaced in the source file from which the PDF was created.

Because text edits are very common, the second row of the Annotations panel contains tools for five types of text edits. You can always find out the name of each tool by holding the pointer over a tool until its name appears in a tool tip.

Tip: To quickly cross out text without switching to a text edit tool, simply highlight text with the Selection tool and press Delete.

1 In the Annotations panel in the Comment pane, select the Replace tool, which is the second tool from the left in the second row.

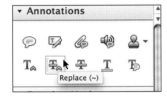

2 Select the word DAY in the NEW DAY RISING headline, and type your replacement text (we wrote: **DAWN**). As you start typing, the pop-up note window should open to show the replacement text you're indicating in this annotation.

3 For the purpose of this exercise there is no need to save any changes to your review work—just close the Local_Magazine_start_cover.pdf file.

The Annotations panel provides you with a variety of other tools for text edits. From left to right in the second row, the tools let you insert text without removing any other text, replace text (as you just did in this lesson), cross out text, underline text, and highlight text and add a comment.

Tip: For major editing work, the specialized markup tools are faster, clearer, and easier to use than simply adding a sticky note and describing an edit.

Managing Reviews

Note: RSS (Really Simple Syndication) is used to publish frequently updated content (e.g., news headlines, blog entries, or podcasts). The RSS format is compatible with XML and RDF formats.

In a managed review, a wizard will help you set up your review and invite the participants. The Tracker, as its name implies, helps you to keep track of the review. The Tracker lets you manage document reviews and enables you to distribute forms as well as administer RSS feeds (online subscriptions to updated content). There's no need for you to import comments, enable commenting for Reader users, or manually track reviewers' responses. To initiate a review, see the sidebar "Initiating a shared review from the Tracker" later in this lesson.

Even if you did not initiate a shared review but are merely a participant, published comments on your local hard drive are synchronized with the comments on the server. You are notified whenever new comments are published—even when the PDF file is closed, because synchronization continues.

Working with the Tracker

Because you might not be connected to the Internet or have e-mail access on your computer, let's just imagine for the purposes of this exercise that you did initiate the cover review—though your Tracker dialog box will look different from the illustration. Some of the settings for the Tracker can be specified in the Acrobat Preferences dialog box.

1 In the Comment pane, expand the Review panel if needed, and then click Send for Shared Review. (To open the Tracker in Adobe Reader, choose View > Tracker.) In the left panel, we were able to select the Local_Magazine_start_cover.pdf under Reviews Sent, because we initiated that review.

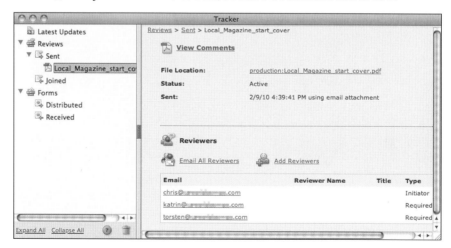

Note: In the Tracker the Sent section lists only the PDF files in reviews you initiated.

Protecting your work

You can use passwords to restrict unauthorized users from opening, printing, or editing a PDF file. You can use a certificate to encrypt a PDF file so that only an approved list of users can open it. If you want to save security settings for later use, you can create a security policy to store your security settings.

By adding security to documents, you can limit viewing, editing, printing, and other options to specified users. You can choose if you prefer the users to have a password, a digital ID, or access to Adobe LiveCycle Rights Management.

Security methods

Acrobat provides a variety of security methods for specifying document encryption and permission settings. You can encrypt all or part of a document and limit user actions. For example, you can allow users to input only in form fields or prevent them from printing a PDF file.

Each security method offers a different set of benefits. However, they all allow you to specify encryption algorithms, choose the document components that you want to encrypt, and set different permissions for different users. Use the Document Properties dialog box to choose one of the following security methods:

- **Password security** provides a simple way to share documents among users when sharing passwords is possible or when backward compatibility is required. Password policies do not require you to specify document recipients.

- **Certificate security** provides a high level of security, eliminates the need for password sharing, and allows you to assign different permissions to different users. Also, you can verify and manage individual user identities.

- **Adobe LiveCycle Rights Management policies** are stored on a server, and users must have access to the server to use them. To create these policies, you specify the document recipients from a list on Adobe LiveCycle Rights Management.

For more information regarding security, refer to Acrobat Help.

When you're an active reviewer, the left panel of the Tracker dialog box displays more details about the reviews, forms, server status messages, and RSS feeds should you want to participate in those. The Latest Updates panel gives you a summary of all the latest changes to reviews in which you are a participant. You can turn Tracker notifications on or off in Acrobat and, for Windows only, in the system tray.

The right panel shows the review details for the item selected in the left panel—in our case the magazine cover review. Because published comments on your local hard drive are synchronized with the comments on the server, you'll be notified automatically when new comments are available.

Initiating a shared review from the Tracker

Although the lesson shows you how to start a shared review using Send for Shared Review, you can also start a shared review if you're already in the Tracker.

1   In the Comment pane, expand the Review panel if needed, and click Track Reviews.

2   When the Tracker dialog box appears, click Create a Shared Review.

If this is the first time you've initiated a shared review, a dialog box will appear asking you to create your own user account at Acrobat.com. This account can be set up from either Acrobat or Reader and enables you to upload and share large documents in most common formats, and also to share your desktop in online meetings.

If you are already participating in reviews using the Tracker, the Tracker dialog box displays more details about those reviews, as well as forms, server status messages, and RSS feeds.

Once the wizard has guided you through setting up the review, you can enter an e-mail list of reviewers and invite them to participate.

▶ **Tip:** To look at the comments from the Tracker, click View Comments to go straight to the sticky notes in the Acrobat document window. At any time during a review the initiator can invite more reviewers by clicking Add Reviewers and entering their e-mail addresses.

2   Right-click / Control-click the file Local_Magazine_start_cover.pdf in the left panel of the Tracker, and choose E-mail All Reviewers. This is a quick way to contact all the other reviewers.

3   You can close the e-mail window when it appears, because there is no need to write a message.

4   As the initiator, you can discontinue a shared review by Right-clicking / Control-clicking the PDF file and choosing End Review.

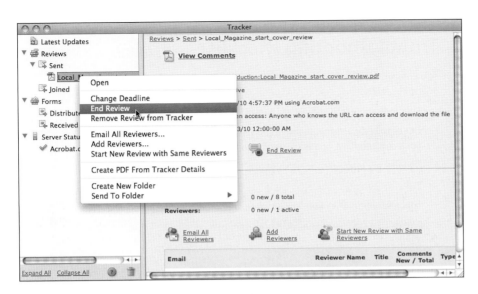

Once a review has ended, participants cannot publish comments to the server. You can allow the review to continue by extending the deadline.

Collaborating in Online Meetings

There may be times when you want to hold an online meeting that involves more than one document or application. In these cases you can't use the shared review described earlier in the lesson, because that's based on a single document. Instead, you can use Adobe ConnectNow, a personal web-conference tool that allows you to conduct real-time meetings—sharing a document or your entire desktop and using live chat, online whiteboards, and other collaborative features. As an attendee, you join the meeting by signing in to an online meeting space using a web browser on your computer.

The great thing about this kind of online meeting is that everybody has the same view, which is set up by the person conducting the meeting. As the initiator, you have complete control of what your clients or colleagues are seeing while you walk them through the project.

▶ **Tip:** Although Acrobat is the example used in this lesson ConnectNow shared meetings aren't limited to Acrobat. You can use ConnectNow to share any file or application on your computer.

Troubleshooting checklist

This checklist may help if you encounter difficulties setting up or attending an online conference:

- Ensure that you are connected to the Internet.
- Check that your software and hardware meet the system requirements. For a complete list, see www.adobe.com/acom/systemreqs.
- Disable any pop-up blocker software.
- Clear the browser cache.
- Try connecting from another computer.
- Ensure that you have entered the correct URL.
- Try joining the meeting as a registered user or as a guest.
- Confirm that you are using the correct password.

An online meeting can be highly productive when it comes to sharing ideas, discussing detailed issues, and collaborating on a project. As a matter of fact, ConnectNow helped a lot in the writing of this book because the various Adobe product teams were able to demonstrate some of the new features of the Creative Suite live to colleagues who were geographically dispersed. Version control, platform compatibility, and even having the same programs installed are no longer an issue. You can enable video conferencing, send instant messages, and even let another participant take control of the desktop. Interaction takes place in real time, which makes the meeting more personal and more fun.

Working with ConnectNow web conferencing

On the following pages you'll be guided through the process of setting up an online meeting to discuss the magazine cover. To share this document from your desktop, you'll use ConnectNow web conferencing on Acrobat.com. You'll need an active Internet connection to work with Share My Screen. If you're not connected to the Internet, you can still follow some of the steps in this exercise and skip others.

1 Switch back to Adobe Bridge, select your Lessons folder in the Favorites panel, and then navigate to the Lesson07 folder. Double-click the file Local_Magazine_start_cover.pdf, which should open in Acrobat.

2 In your web browser, go to Acrobat.com, and then click Sign In. If you see a pop-up menu, choose Acrobat.com.

3 Enter the e-mail address and password that you use as your Adobe ID, and click Sign In.

If you don't already have an Adobe ID, click Create An Account For Free and when you're done with that, return to step 2.

4 After signing in, click Web Conferencing, and then click Start a Meeting.

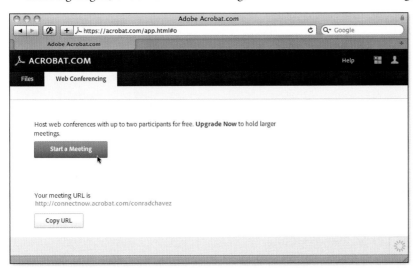

It will take a moment for the server to sign you in; then the Welcome to Your ConnectNow Meeting Room dialog box appears offering you two choices:

- **Customize Your Meeting URL.** The end of the URL is your name by default, but you can change it to something that better describes the nature of the meeting or to a word or phrase that's shorter or easier to remember.

- **Send E-Mail Invitation Now.** This option opens the default e-mail client on your system with a message that contains the URL for your meeting. You'll have an opportunity to edit the message before you send it.

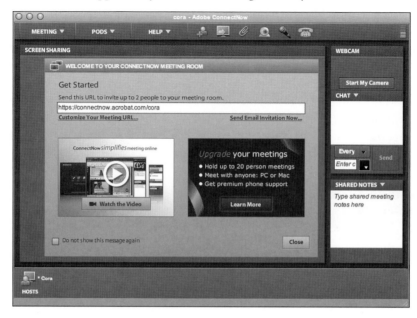

5   If there's someone who can join you for this exercise and that person has installed Acrobat 9 or later or Acrobat Reader 9 or later, you can click Send E-Mail Invitation Now, and that person can be your attendee. Or you can make a note of the URL and click Close.

If you have access to another networked computer, you can enter the URL into a web browser on that computer to see how Share My Screen looks from the point of view of an attendee. Attendees don't need an Adobe ID; they can sign in as a guest, and the meeting host (you) can decide whether to let them in.

6   Click Share My Computer Screen to start the meeting. You may be asked to approve the installation of the Adobe ConnectNow add-in for your web browser; click Yes.

You'll be asked what you want to share—your entire computer desktop, individual windows, or a specific application. When you have windows open with information you don't want the meeting participants to see, it's a good idea to restrict what you display to others, limiting screen sharing to one application or even just one window.

7 Click Windows, and then in the list select Local_Magazine_start_cover.pdf.

While the meeting is in progress, the ConnectNow screen sharing panel is displayed, giving you access to key meeting features and enabling you to share notes, send chat messages to one person or the whole group, use an online whiteboard to sketch ideas, activate a webcam, and even turn over the control of your desktop to another attendee, which can be very productive for collaborative work sessions and technical support. You can position the ConnectNow screen sharing panel wherever you want on your desktop.

▶ **Tip:** To make your messages stand out, you can customize your Chat pod by choosing fonts, sizes, colors, and emoticons.

8 The open Acrobat file on your desktop is now shared with the other participants. Notice the ConnectNow screen sharing panel where you can type chat messages to other attendees and also control various meeting tools, such as your webcam.

9 When an attendee wants to join the meeting, an alert will appear. Click Accept to admit that attendee to the meeting room. The attendee receives a note indicating that the host has been notified of the attendee's presence.

The Chat window is useful for side discussions during the meeting as a way to ask questions and to provide any instructions for the attendees.

10 In the Chat window type a message (such as **Welcome to the meeting**), and then click Send. If you have other attendees set up, you can have them enter a reply.

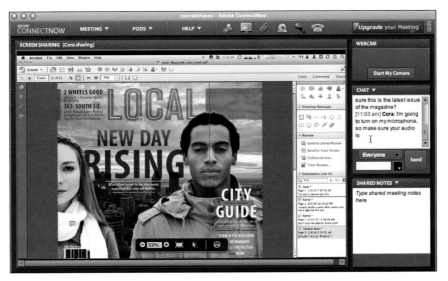

▶ **Tip:** It's possible for a technician to resolve problems directly on your computer, even though the tech is only present online. That's possible with Share My Screen, because you can hand over control of your computer to another participant in the meeting.

11 In the ConnectNow screen sharing panel, click the triangle to the right of the attendee's name and choose Give this user control of my computer.

Being able to work in the application that was used to create the artwork is beneficial because you or any trusted reviewer can quickly react to a suggestion. For example, it would take you only a couple of seconds to demonstrate how the cover would look with a different headline.

12 To leave the online conference, click Exit Adobe ConnectNow. You're given an opportunity to customize the goodbye message that attendees see.

Bravo! You finished the online review and with it the last lesson in this book. You've covered a lot of ground: from creating basic assets to publishing a magazine in both printed and interactive form—from prototyping and building a website and designing for mobile devices to experimenting with different review workflows. There is so much more that you can do with Adobe Creative Suite 6 Design & Web Premium—this is just the beginning!

About approval workflows

For some PDF reviews, you might only need to get a document approved rather than collecting a lot of comments. Acrobat enables you to send a PDF file as an e-mail attachment for others to approve—even in Chinese, Japanese, and Korean!

When participants open an approval request in Acrobat, they can approve the PDF by adding a digital identity stamp from the Sign & Certify panel in the Tools pane.

They can then send the PDF to others for approval via e-mail or return the PDF to the initiator and other appropriate participants. The initiator can track progress by choosing to be notified each time the PDF is approved. The workflow ends when the last participant adds the final approval. If a PDF isn't approved, the approval workflow must be started again.

Review Questions

1   What are the advantages of the shared review using a centralized server?

2   Describe three of Acrobat's comment or markup tools, and explain where to find them.

3   Describe three ways to review a PDF file online.

Review Answers

1   Using a centralized server allows all participants to collaborate directly with each other rather than only through the initiator. Not only can they read and reply to each others' comments, but they also receive notifications when new comments are published.

2   The comment and markup tools in Acrobat can be accessed by expanding the Annotations and Drawing Markups panels in the Comment pane. These tools enable you to make edits, attach notes, and even draw diagrams to communicate your ideas or provide feedback for a PDF file being reviewed. Using the Sticky Note tool you can add your comments in the form of a yellow note icon that appears on the page with a pop-up note for your text. With the text edit tools you can make a variety of edits, such as replacing text, highlighting, underlining, or adding a note to selected text. You can insert text, or cross it out for deletion. The Stamp tool enables you to apply a stamp to a PDF in much the same way you apply a rubber stamp to a paper document. You can apply predefined stamps or create custom stamps.

3   An e-mail-based review lets you manage a review without a central server. With an e-mail review you're the only person who sees all of the comments. A shared review lets you host a review on a central server so that reviewers can view and respond to each others' comments. A live, collaborative review lets you and your reviewers view a document simultaneously online with the option of a chat session, and a ConnectNow meeting adds the ability to share anything on your computer, not just one document.

8 PREPARING IMAGES FOR DIFFERENT MEDIA

In this lesson you'll learn how to intelligently prepare and manage images for use across different media:

- Understanding the multiple meanings of resolution and how they apply to different media

- Adjusting image size as you crop

- Sharpening images for different media

- Preparing image color for different media

- Inspecting and changing image resolution in various Adobe software applications

 You'll probably need between one and two hours to complete this lesson.

Learn how to optimize the size, resolution, and color
of a source image so that it reproduces well in print,
on the web, and on mobile devices.

One Image, Multiple Paths

An image today can be reproduced in many different ways. Unlike the time when an image's only destiny was to be printed on a press, now an image can also be shown on a website or displayed in a video. These media have very different reproduction requirements, so if you want your images to look their best, use Adobe Creative Suite 6 Design & Web Premium to properly optimize versions of an image for different media. For example, it's important to prepare images for a website at a size that's appropriate for the connection speed of the site's audience so that the website loads quickly. Preparing images in the correct color space helps ensure that image colors are spot on.

When you prepare an image for output on only one device, such as a press, you can simply edit the image as needed and archive it when the job is done. But when you know an image will be used in multiple media, you need to do a little more advance planning. Every output device—from a press to a tablet to an inkjet printer—has its own capabilities and limitations, so optimizing an image for one specific device may make it work less well on other devices. For example, if you convert an RGB image to CMYK color for a printing press, and then later create a copy of that CMYK image for the web, its colors may appear dull compared to if you had created a web version from the original RGB image. Similarly, taking a low-resolution image from a website and printing it on a printing press may result in a coarse-looking image due to inadequate resolution. In both cases, the best solution is to produce each media-specific version from the original, or master, image. The master image can be a camera raw image or a digital negative (DNG) file if all necessary corrections were completed in Adobe Camera Raw, or it can be a layered Photoshop document containing your edits. If the image is a graphic drawn from scratch, it can also be an Adobe Illustrator (AI) document or an Adobe Fireworks (PNG) document.

Adobe Creative Suite 6 Design & Web Premium is built to help you optimize images for different media. You can use Adobe Photoshop, Adobe Illustrator, and Adobe Fireworks to easily export a web-optimized duplicate of an image that leaves the master (original) image untouched.

Image Resolution and Media

The number of pixels you send to a printer or a screen affects your production efficiency and your viewer's experience. Send an image with too few pixels and the image looks coarse and blocky. Send too many pixels and you'll slow downloading, viewing, and printing. Fortunately, Adobe Creative Suite 6 Design & Web Premium provides ways to inspect and adjust resolution while preserving quality.

Understanding the multiple meanings of resolution

In digital design, the term resolution is used in different ways:

- As pixel dimensions, such as 1024 x 768 pixels. This is typically used for onscreen media such as web and video, as well as for cameras. You'll probably also recognize this usage from the specifications for computer and video displays; for example, 1920 x 1080 pixels is the display size for 1080p HD televisions.

- As a measure of pixel or printed dot density, such as 300 pixels per inch. Expressing resolution as a ratio is typically done when referring to printed output. However, it's starting to work its way into discussions of displays such as tablets and smartphones as their pixel density approaches that of print, for instance the 326 ppi display of the iPhone 4S. Thinking of resolution this way requires both horizontal and vertical pixel dimensions, as well as a physical measurement, such as inches. For more information, see the sidebar "Preparing graphics for high-resolution displays" later in this lesson.

- As megapixels. This is simply the number of pixels in an image expressed in millions of pixels; 1 megapixel is 1 million pixels. You usually see resolution expressed as megapixels in the specifications for digital cameras. Megapixels are directly related to the pixel dimensions of the images produced by a digital camera, so it's easy to work out the megapixel resolution of any image. For example, to find out how many megapixels are in a digital camera image that's 4500 x 3000 pixels, simply multiply the two dimensions: 4500 times 3000 equals 13,500,000 pixels, or 13.5 megapixels.

▶ **Tip:** The abbreviations ppi (pixels per inch) and dpi (dots per inch) are both used to describe resolution as pixel density. Generally, ppi is used when measuring pixels (picture elements) in an image file or on a monitor, whereas dpi is generally used when referring to dots on printed output.

In conversation, these different meanings for resolution can cause confusion, so keep these differences in mind as you work in various media. Later in this lesson you'll learn how to inspect images for both pixel dimensions and density.

Typical media resolutions

As you prepare images for various media, what resolutions should you aim for? This overview provides some guidelines for sizing images for various media, and later in this lesson you'll adjust an image to various media sizes.

Online media

When you're designing for onscreen media, such as websites, video programs, or mobile devices, you'll want to determine the space available to the image in the design as expressed in pixel dimensions. In conventional web design, the pixel dimensions of a web page are based on the pixel dimensions of the typical display used by the target audience, and the pixel dimensions of individual images are designed to fit within that layout. For example, a web designer might design based on an assumption that a site will be viewed mostly on netbook displays that are 1024 pixels wide.

However, that practice is rapidly changing as more sites accommodate mobile devices, which have a very wide range of screen sizes. It's no longer practical to assume one or two primary screen sizes. Web designers are moving toward modular page designs that can automatically recompose themselves into smaller yet still readable chunks based on columns, as you saw in Lesson 5, Building a Website. It is increasingly likely that the pixel dimensions of web graphics will fit into these smaller chunks so that they can display as effectively on mobile device displays as they do on desktop displays.

Video projects, such as the kind you can create in Adobe Photoshop, still use fixed frame sizes. If you want an image to fill the screen, determine the pixel dimensions of the video standard, and then resize or crop the image as needed. For example, if you're creating a 720p HD video, you should create images that match the 1280 x 720 pixel dimensions of that video standard.

Printed media

The resolution requirements for printed media are not always straightforward. Just because an inkjet printer creates output at 2880 dpi does not mean you should save images at 2880 dpi; in fact, it's very unlikely that you would because most printing technologies create colors and tones by combining printer dots into larger cells or patterns. In general, you'll find the following guidelines to be helpful:

- For general office use or for documents you'll photocopy, it's usually best to use image resolutions between 150 and 300 dpi.

- For prepress or fine-art printing, images are typically reproduced at 240 to 360 dpi. However, the more expensive the job, the more you'll want to consult with your prepress service provider before committing to the job to find out what resolution you should target when preparing images, based on the specific printing system your service provider uses.

- Viewing distance can affect resolution requirements. For example, a roadside billboard or large banner can be printed at 100 dpi because it won't be seen up close. An image's pixel density of 150 dpi at arm's length becomes an effective pixel density of 300 dpi simply by doubling the viewing distance. Your service provider can advise you on the optimum resolution for the printing medium and viewing distance of your job.

Image Color and Media

Different media have varying color requirements:

- Online media use color specified using the RGB color mode, either as RGB values (such as red 108, green 18, and blue 172) or a hexidecimal value (#6c12ac).

- Printed media intended for a press typically uses color specified using the CMYK color mode (such as cyan 72%, magenta 95%, yellow 0%, black 0%).

- Although printing ink is typically based on the CMYK color mode, some printing processes may expect to receive color specified using the RGB color mode if the conversion to CMYK will happen after the job is sent to the printer, for example, when colors are converted by the printer driver behind the scenes. This is the case with most desktop inkjet printers and some on-demand presses.

Within a color mode, multiple color spaces are possible. Color spaces are variations commonly based on the particular color range that a display or print device can actually reproduce. You can read a more complete explanation of color management in Lesson 10, but for this lesson, you'll convert online RGB colors to the sRGB color space, which is a standard for both the web and computer monitors. You'll also convert print colors to a generic CMYK color space—although for an actual print job you'd convert CMYK color to the color space of a specific press standard.

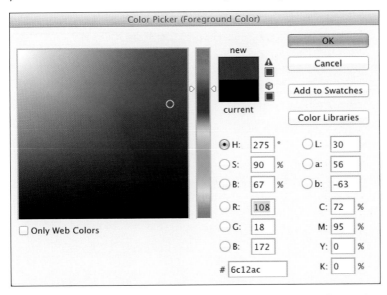

The color picker in Adobe Photoshop lets you specify color values in different color modes, including HSB (Hue, Saturation, Brightness), RGB, hexadecimal for the web, and CMYK.

Preparing Graphics for the Web or Mobile Devices

Now you'll walk through preparing an image for online media. The image starts out as a DNG (digital negative) file from a digital camera. You'll make the necessary corrections to size, resolution, and color.

Exporting images for online media using only Bridge and Camera Raw

For this part of the lesson, you'll create a graphic that's 240 pixels wide and 320 pixels tall to fit in a mobile-friendly web page layout.

1   In Adobe Bridge, navigate to the Lesson08 folder in your Lessons folder.

2   Select the file Fireplace_Closeup.dng.

3   If the Metadata panel isn't visible, choose Window > Metadata Panel.

In the Metadata panel, note the Dimensions, Color Mode, and Color Profile sections. The Dimensions are the pixel dimensions, the Color Mode is RGB, and the Color Profile is "Untagged" because it's a camera raw file. The Metadata panel in Adobe Bridge is a great way to check file specifications without opening them.

Now you'll take the steps necessary to meet the specifications from the website.

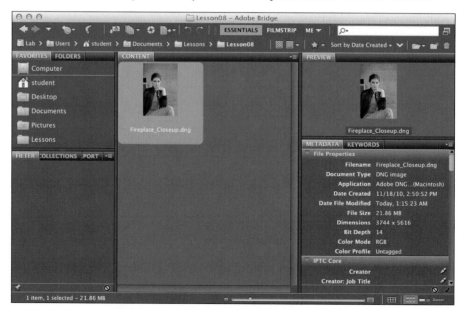

4   Choose File > Open in Camera Raw.

This lesson concentrates on the production aspects of the image, not basic image correction, so you won't make other adjustments in Camera Raw. You'll set up options that affect the conversion to Photoshop and then proceed directly to Photoshop.

5   Click the underlined link text at the bottom of the Camera Raw dialog box.

6   In the Workflow Options dialog box that appears, set Space to sRGB, set Depth to 8 Bits/Channel, leave Size and Resolution unchanged (more on that in a moment), and for the Sharpen For option, select Screen.

The Workflow Options dialog box has no immediate effect on the raw file: It affects the conversion to another format, such as when you open the raw file in Photoshop or save directly from Camera Raw.

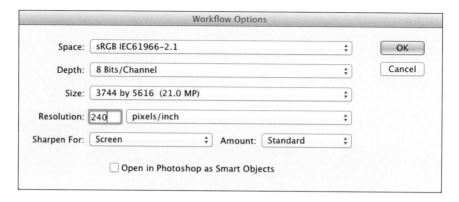

7   Click OK.

8   Hold the mouse on the Crop tool () and choose Custom from the Crop
    tool menu.

9   In the Custom Crop dialog box that appears, choose Pixels from the Crop menu,
    enter **320** by **240**, and click OK.

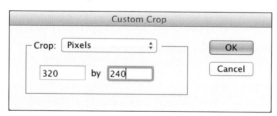

10 Using the Crop tool, drag a crop rectangle around the model, and press Enter/
Return.

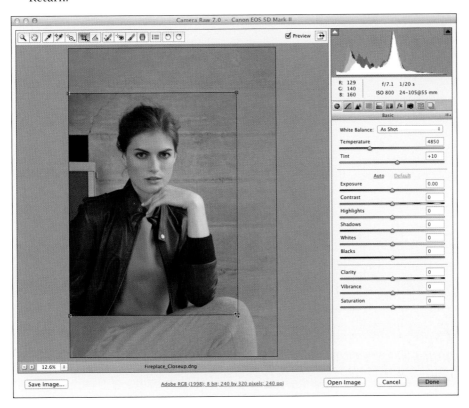

11 Click the Save Image button, and in the Save Options dialog box, do the
following:

- Click the Select Folder button and set the location to your Lesson08 folder.

- For File Naming, choose Document Name for the first field, and enter **_web**
for the second field.

- Choose JPEG from the Format menu.

- Set Quality to High (8-9).

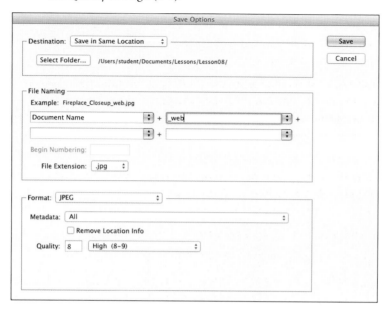

12 Click Save to close the Save Options dialog box.

13 Click Done. In Adobe Bridge select the Fireplace_Closeup_web.jpg image you just saved.

14 In the Metadata panel, notice that the Dimensions are 240 by 320 pixels because of your Crop tool settings, and the Color Profile is sRGB because of your Workflow Options settings.

And even though you left the Workflow Options dialog box set to the image's original pixel dimensions (3744 by 5616 pixels), the final dimensions were dictated by your Crop tool settings of 240 by 320 pixels.

You might also have noticed that the Resolution setting in Workflow Options was left at 240 ppi and remained that way in Adobe Bridge. Most websites and mobile devices don't use a ppi or dpi resolution value; instead, it's the pixel dimensions that are important. So, for online media full-screen it typically doesn't matter what ppi value you use.

15 Press the spacebar to display your web image in full-screen view. Press the left arrow key to view the DNG file you cropped; it will look less sharp because of the sharpening you applied in the Save dialog box.

16 Press the spacebar to close the full-screen view.

Exporting images for online media using Photoshop

In the previous example, you were able to crop an image to specific pixel dimensions and set its color space to sRGB using Adobe Camera Raw without entering Photoshop. If the edits you need can be accomplished by the tools in Camera Raw, you can stay in Adobe Bridge and quickly export web images from Camera Raw. But because you sometimes need to use the additional tools in Photoshop, you'll take a look at that in this section.

1 In Adobe Bridge, select the file Fireplace_Closeup.dng in your Lesson08 folder.

You don't want to create a new version from the optimized JPEG image you just exported, so you'll begin by selecting the full-quality master image.

2   You'll be using the Crop tool in Photoshop, so with Fireplace_Closeup.dng still selected in Adobe Bridge, choose Edit > Develop Settings > Clear Settings to revert the raw file to its original state. The image regains the area you cropped out earlier, because cropping in Camera Raw isn't a permanent change.

3   With the image still selected, press Enter/Return. This time, instead of opening in Camera Raw hosted by Adobe Bridge, the file opens in Camera Raw hosted by Photoshop. If Photoshop isn't already open, it may take a few seconds to load.

4   Click the underlined link text at the bottom of the Camera Raw dialog box. You'll use slightly different settings this time because you'll be cropping and sizing in Photoshop instead of Camera Raw.

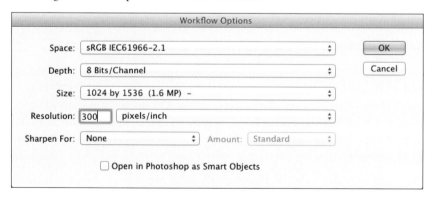

Preparing graphics for high-resolution displays

New displays are capable of resolutions in the range formerly achieved only by print. For example, as of this writing the iPad display has a pixel density of 264 ppi, and the iPhone 4S display has a pixel density of 326 ppi (higher than some desktop printers). The old wisdom of assuming that displays are 72 to 120 ppi no longer holds. How does this change the way you prepare images for the new high-resolution displays?

It isn't a good idea to simply replace all your online images with images having a high pixel density. The larger files will significantly increase page loading time on slower Internet connections without improving image quality on displays with a more traditional pixel density.

It's possible to use media queries, discussed in Lesson 3, to have your website code identify the screen resolution of a device, and then use JavaScript code to send up an image with the appropriate number of pixels. However, knowing the pixel density of the display isn't enough: A high-resolution display may be on a slow connection, such as cellular data, where sending large images will degrade the viewer's experience. You'll need to consult with your website developer to see if an automatic image replacement solution is practical to implement for your website.

For line art, logos, and other graphics that can be represented as vector art, consider using the SVG (Scalable Vector Graphics) file format if you know that your audience uses browsers that support SVG. Vector graphics are compact and can be enlarged without increasing file size, so they're very bandwidth-efficient. You can use Adobe Illustrator to create vector graphics and save them in SVG format, and you can integrate SVG-format graphics into your website using Adobe Dreamweaver.

For type, avoid creating type as a bitmap image, because that locks the image of the type to a specific resolution—the type won't look good if it's significantly enlarged. Instead, plan to use web fonts, such as those available through TypeKit by Adobe (typekit.com). Web fonts are served as vector type, so like with vector graphics, you can use web fonts at any size on a display of any resolution and they'll always look perfectly sharp on supported browsers.

5   In the Workflow Options dialog box, do the following:

   •   Leave the Space at sRGB and the Depth at 8 Bits/Channel.

   •   Because you only need a 320-by-240-pixel image, choose the smallest Size
       setting, 1024 x 1536 (1.6 MP). By converting fewer pixels, Photoshop will
       work faster and use less memory.

   •   Set the Resolution to 300 pixels/inch.

   •   In the Sharpen For menu, choose None. You could leave it set to Screen if
       you did not plan to sharpen any further, but typically output sharpening
       should be left as the last step, and Photoshop has more sharpening options
       than Camera Raw.

6   Click OK to close the Workflow Options dialog box

7   Click Open Image.

8   Choose View > Rulers. If they're currently set to inches, right-click/Control-
    click a ruler and choose Pixels.

9   Select the Crop tool. In the Options bar, enter dimensions of **240 px** x **320 px**.
    Typing **px** after the dimension value tells Photoshop to use pixels as the unit of
    measure for the crop rectangle.

10 Adjust any side or corner of the crop rectangle until the image is properly composed, and then press Enter/Return.

11 Choose View > Actual Pixels to see the image at 1:1 magnification.

12 Click the status bar at the bottom of the document window. You can use this display to confirm that the document dimensions are correct.

▶ **Tip:** To permanently display the dimensions of a document in the status bar, click the triangle to the right of the status bar and choose Document Dimensions.

Tip: In the Smart Sharpen dialog box, you can compare the sharpening settings to the unsharpened image in two ways. Select the Preview check box (or press P) to toggle between the sharpened and unsharpened images in the document window, or hold down the mouse on the preview inside the Smart Sharpen dialog box.

13 Choose Filter > Sharpen > Smart Sharpen, choose Lens Blur from the Remove menu, and adjust Amount and Radius until the image is pleasingly sharpened. You can use the settings in the following figure as a guideline.

14 When you're done, click OK to close the Smart Sharpen dialog box.

Tip: You'll also find the Save for Web dialog box in Adobe Illustrator.

15 Choose File > Save for Web. You'll find that this dialog box gives you more options than the Save dialog box in Camera Raw.

16 In the Save for Web dialog box, do the following and then click Save:

- Click the 2-Up tab, and choose JPEG High from the Preset menu.

- Examine the Original and JPEG tabs to make sure the image appearance and file size are acceptable. If they aren't, you can change the optimization settings in the top-right corner of the Save for Web dialog box.

- Make sure Convert to sRGB is selected to ensure that whatever the original color space was it will be properly converted for online media here.

- Look at the Image Size options to verify they're correct. The Image Size options are an alternate way to resize an image if the image is already cropped to the correct proportions.

17 Click Save to close the Save for Web dialog box.

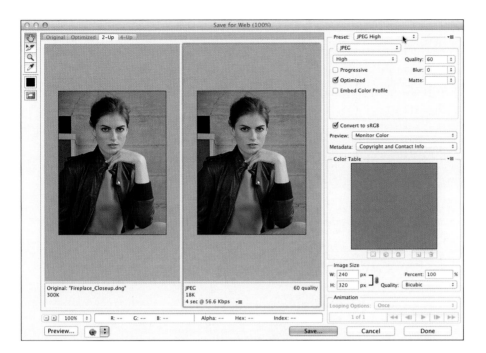

Tip: if you want to compare specific images in full-screen mode, select them before pressing the spacebar so that they are the only images you'll cycle through. If you want to see images side by side, select them and make the Preview panel larger.

18 Click the Save button, and in the Save Optimized As dialog box, navigate to your Lesson08 folder, name the file **Fireplace_Closeup_web2.jpg**, and click Save. If you see a compatibility warning about filename characters, click OK to accept it.

19 Close the Photoshop document. When asked if you want to save changes, click Save, name it **Fireplace_Closeup_web2.psd**, and save it to your Lesson08 folder.

20 Switch to Adobe Bridge, select the Fireplace_Closeup_web2.jpg, and press the spacebar to view it full screen. You can compare it to the other JPEG image you exported earlier.

You've tried two ways to prepare an image for online media: editing through Camera Raw and editing through Photoshop, and in both cases you used Adobe Bridge to inspect images before editing and to verify them after editing.

Inspecting image size in Dreamweaver

When you import an image into Dreamweaver, you can easily check its size and resize it if needed.

1 Start Dreamweaver, and in the Create New section of the Welcome Screen, click HTML.

2 Position the Dreamweaver and Adobe Bridge windows so that you can see both.

3 Switch to Adobe Bridge, and drag one of the JPEG images you exported into the Design view on the right side of the split Dreamweaver window. Click OK or Save in any dialog boxes that follow; Dreamweaver is ensuring that the image is copied within the folder structure of the site.

4 With the image selected, notice that there are width (W) and height (H) options in the Properties panel at the bottom of the Dreamweaver window. You can use these options to verify image dimensions when you design a web page. You can also change these values to resize an image on a layout, but this is not as optimal as resizing the image in Adobe Photoshop or Adobe Fireworks.

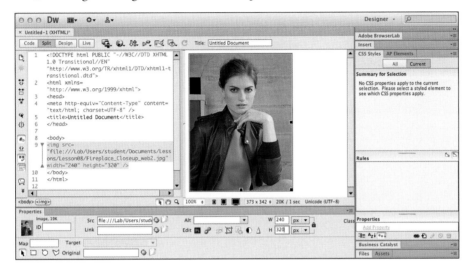

5 Exit Dreamweaver. When asked to save changes, click Don't Save.

You'll find a similar Properties panel in Adobe Fireworks, and in Adobe Flash you'd check the image size in the Position and Size panel.

Preparing Graphics for Print

Now you'll walk through preparing the same DNG image for a job going to press, making necessary corrections to size, resolution, and color.

Exporting images for print media using Photoshop

For this part of the lesson, you'll create a graphic that's 2-inches wide and 3-inches tall to fit in a page layout for printed output.

1 In Adobe Bridge, select the file Fireplace_Closeup.dng in the Lesson08 folder in your Lessons folder, and press Enter/Return to open it in Camera Raw hosted by Photoshop.

Again, to create a new version at optimal quality, you start from the original, not from any of the derivative JPEG versions you've already created.

2 Click the underlined link text at the bottom of the Camera Raw dialog box.

3 In the Workflow Options dialog box that appears, do the following:

- Set Space to Adobe RGB, which better accommodates the range of colors in the CMYK color mode into which the image will be converted later in Photoshop.

- Set Depth to 8 Bits/Channel.

- Set Size to 3744 by 5616 (21.0 MP). Note that this is the one option in the Size menu that doesn't have a minus or plus sign after it. This means it's the native size of the image—Camera Raw won't enlarge or reduce it.

- Set Resolution to **300** pixels/inch.

- Set the Sharpen For menu to None.

4 Click OK to close the Workflow Options dialog box.

As in the earlier example for online media, this lesson concentrates on the production aspects of the image, not basic image correction, so you won't make other adjustments in Camera Raw; you'll proceed directly to Photoshop.

5 Click Open Image to convert the raw image into Adobe Photoshop format using the settings in the Workflow Options dialog box.

6 If the rulers aren't visible, choose View > Rulers to display them. If the rulers display in pixel units, right-click/Control-click the rulers and choose Inches from the context menu that appears.

7   Select the Crop tool. The Options bar probably retained the settings you entered earlier for online images; you'll need to change those now.

8   In the Options bar, choose Size & Resolution from the Crop tool options menu, and do the following:

   •   Set the Width and Height menus to Inches.

   •   Enter a Width of **2**, a Height of **3**, and a Resolution of **300** Pixels/Inch.

   •   Select Save as Crop Preset.

Creating a new crop preset means that if you need to use the Crop tool with the same settings in the future, you can simply choose that preset from the Crop tool options menu.

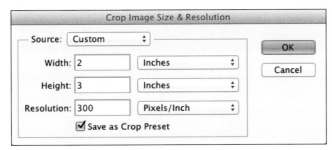

9   Click OK.

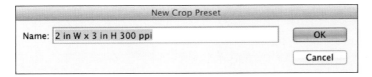

10 Adjust any side or corner of the crop rectangle until the image is properly composed, and then press Enter/Return.

11 Choose View > Fit on Screen to see the entire image.

For the web image you created earlier, you used the View > Actual Pixels command, but the pixel dimensions of this image are so much higher that on some monitors Actual Pixels may be too large for the display.

Tip: To permanently display the dimensions of a document in the status bar, click the triangle to the right of the status bar and choose Document Dimensions.

12 Click the status bar at the bottom of the document window to confirm that the document dimensions are 2 by 3 inches and the resolution is 300 ppi. The Crop tool accomplished both resizing and setting the resolution in one step.

13 Choose Filter > Sharpen > Smart Sharpen, choose Lens Blur from the Remove menu, and adjust Amount and Radius until the image is pleasingly sharpened. You can use the settings in the following figure as a guideline.

You might notice that the settings are much higher than they were for the online media image you prepared earlier. The higher pixel density of printed output requires that you apply more sharpening for the effect to be visible. For actual press runs, it's best to run tests in advance to determine the appropriate level of sharpening, because you can't reliably preview printed sharpening onscreen.

14 When you're done, click OK to close the Smart Sharpen dialog box.

The image is currently in RGB color mode, which you can verify by viewing the menu that appears when you click the status bar. But the job requires converting the image to CMYK color mode, which you'll do now.

15 Choose Edit > Convert to Profile, and in the Destination Space menu, choose U.S. Web Coated (SWOP) v2. This may also appear at the top of the menu as Working CMYK – U.S. Web Coated (SWOP) v2, and you may choose that option as well. Leave the other settings at their defaults, as shown in the following figure. Click OK.

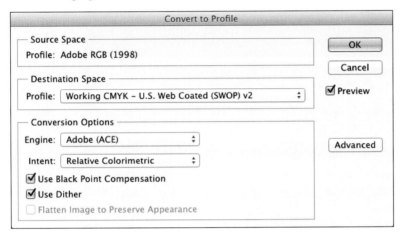

On an actual CMYK print job, it's likely that your prepress service provider would provide a CMYK profile for you to install so that it appears in the Destination Space menu. You would then choose that specific profile instead of the generic one you chose for this lesson. Using a specially tailored CMYK profile helps ensure that colors are converted properly for the specific press on which the job will be printed.

16 Choose File > Save As, navigate to your Lesson08 folder, name the file **Fireplace_Closeup_CMYK.psd**, and click Save. Close the document window.

Some older workflows may require you to save the image in TIFF format, but recent versions of Adobe InDesign can directly import Photoshop format (PSD) image files.

Inspecting an Image in Adobe InDesign

When you import an image into Adobe InDesign, you can easily check its size, resolution, and other attributes.

1 Start Adobe InDesign.

2 In the Create New section on the Welcome Screen, click Document.

3 In the New Document dialog box, make sure [Default] is selected as the Document Preset and click OK.

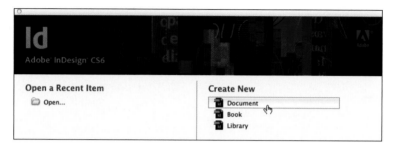

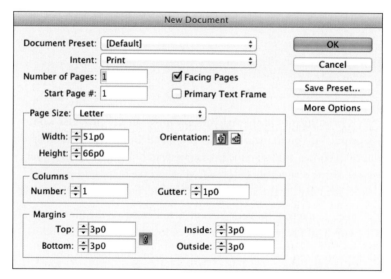

4 Position the InDesign and Adobe Bridge windows so that you can see both.

5 Switch to Adobe Bridge, and drag the PSD image you saved into the InDesign layout. Click the loaded place icon anywhere on the layout.

Tip: The Info panel displays the color profile of the CMYK image used in this lesson because the profile was set to be embedded in the Save As dialog box in Photoshop. In some CMYK workflows, your prepress service provider may ask you to not embed the CMYK profile, so be sure to ask.

6 With the image selected, notice that there are width (W) and height (H) options in the Control panel at the top of the InDesign workspace. You can change these values to resize an image on a layout.

7 If the Info panel isn't visible, choose Window > Info. It tells you the file type, Actual and Effective ppi, and the image's current color space and color profile.

(If you still can't see the ppi readout in the Info panel, make sure the image is selected, and in the Info panel choose Show Options from the Info panel menu.)

The Info panel lists Actual and Effective ppi because pixel density on a print layout depends on its physical dimensions on the page. Enlarging lowers the pixel density; reducing increases pixel density.

Tip: To view images at full resolution, make sure View > Display Performance > High Quality Display is selected. High Quality Display takes more time to redraw, so the three Display Performance options let you balance screen display speed and quality.

8 Ctrl-Shift-drag/Command-Shift-drag any corner handle of the image outward to enlarge the image on the layout. (If the image doesn't enlarge, choose Edit > Undo and try again, but this time hold down the two keys before dragging the handle.)

Notice that in the Info panel the Effective ppi is now lower than the Actual ppi to show that you're stretching the same number of pixels across a larger area, lowering the pixel density. Your prepress service provider can help you figure out the lowest acceptable Effective ppi for your print job.

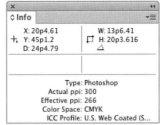

When you're getting ready to send out a print job, you don't have to check the specs of each image using the Info panel. The Preflight feature lets you verify all images in the document at once. You used the Preflight feature in Lesson 2.

Remember that you can use Adobe Bridge to check the specifications of images outside of InDesign or Dreamweaver.

Wrapping Up

Congratulations! You've walked through key steps in properly inspecting and setting image size and resolution for printed and online media using several Adobe Creative Suite 6 Design & Web Premium software applications.

Review questions

1 What are the three different ways that the term resolution is used in digital media?

2 In Adobe Bridge, which panel is useful for inspecting pixel dimensions, pixel density, and other specifications of a selected image?

3 Why can't the same sharpening settings apply to both online and printed images?

4 When converting image colors to CMYK, which profile is best for printing to a press?

5 In Adobe InDesign, what is the difference between Actual ppi and Effective ppi?

Review answers

1 The term resolution is used when referring to the pixel dimensions of an image or display, the pixel density (ppi or dpi), and camera megapixels.

2 In Adobe Bridge you can use the Metadata panel to inspect image resolution and other specifications for a selected image.

3 The effectiveness of sharpening settings is affected by pixel density, and printed images typically require much higher pixel density than online images.

4 The best CMYK profile to use for a job printed to a press is the profile recommended by your prepress service provider.

5 Actual ppi is the pixel density of the image as it was saved; Effective ppi describes how pixel density is changed after you resize an image on a page layout.

9 MANAGING COLOR ACROSS ADOBE CREATIVE SUITE

Lesson Overview

In this lesson, you'll learn how to achieve consistent color across Adobe Creative Suite 6 Design & Web Premium workflows:

- Understanding color management fundamentals

- Improving output by using accurate color profiles

- Setting up a color-managed print workflow

- Setting up a web color workflow

- Using profiles to convert colors between color spaces

 You'll probably need between one and two hours to complete this lesson.

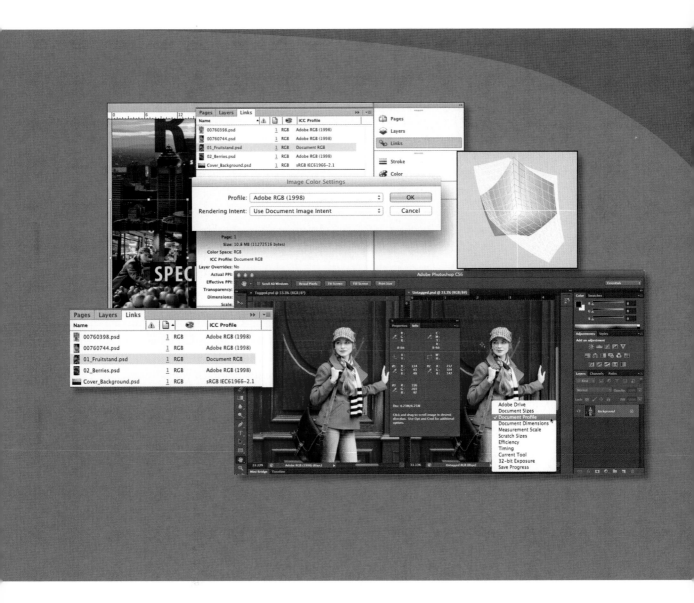

Learn how to set up Adobe Creative Suite so that colors remain consistent as you move among applications.

Understanding Color Management

The challenge of reproducing color consistently is that it isn't possible to make all kinds of output reproduce color in the same way. The range of colors that can be reproduced varies depending on the specific technologies, inks, and materials that are used, from computer displays to smartphones to ink on paper. There's a lot of variation even within individual categories; for instance, ten different models of computer displays will reproduce ten different ranges of color, and the same is true for ten different combinations of ink and paper.

Color management is a technology that makes color reproduction more consistent across many types of devices and forms of output. For example, you can use color management to help you preview how closely a printing press can reproduce the colors you use in Adobe InDesign and see on your monitor, and to convert the colors of a photograph so that they reproduce consistently across print, web, and other media.

Color management helps reproduce color consistently by translating color among the parts of your workflow, including documents, applications, and devices. It gets information about your workflow from color profiles, which you'll read about later in this lesson.

● **Note:** Although color management can work out how to make colors match between different parts of your workflow, that doesn't mean that match is achievable. For example, you may be able to create and see colors on your display that are outside the range of colors your printer can reproduce. In that case, color management can help you print the closest, but not exact, color.

Adobe Creative Suite software has long supported color management technology, not just in the individual applications but across the suite. Because color management is woven through so many parts of a design and production workflow, it can't be handled in just one place. Instead, you'll encounter bits and pieces of color management throughput your workflow. For that reason, it's useful to know the "big picture" of color management and also recognize the points in your Creative Suite workflow where color management requires attention.

Color modes and color spaces

One of the reasons that various forms of output reproduce different color ranges is that there are two opposite ways to reproduce a color. Self-lit computer displays (such as an LCD monitor) use *additive color*, which uses transmitted light. Printed output (such as a magazine or inkjet print) uses *subtractive color*, which uses reflected light. Both methods build a wide range of colors from just a few *primary colors*. The additive primary colors are red, green, and blue, which is why you specify online colors using RGB color values. The subtractive primary colors are cyan, magenta, and yellow; you see black added to that mix because ink impurities prevent cyan, magenta, and yellow from achieving a dense neutral black on their own.

RGB and CMYK are called *color modes*. Some Adobe Creative Suite applications support other color modes, such as HSB (Hue, Saturation, Brightness), Lab (which represents the Lightness, a*, and b* channels), and gray (just lightness). One of the jobs of color management is to translate colors between color modes while maintaining their appearance as consistently as possible. For instance, this is important when translating colors between the RGB color mode of cameras and displays and the CMYK color mode of print.

Within a single color mode, multiple *color spaces* are possible. For example, glossy photo paper typically has a larger color space than matte paper, which means it reproduces a wider range of colors. When you convert colors in Adobe Creative Suite, for best results you'll always want to be aware of the source and destination color spaces—where the colors are coming from and going to, respectively.

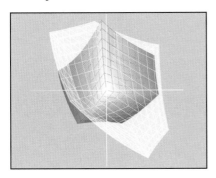

This screen shot from the Apple ColorSync Utility compares the color spaces of sRGB (in color) and a typical CMYK press (in light gray). Not only are the color spaces different sizes, but they are also different shapes, and each color space can reproduce colors the other cannot. Another conclusion you can draw is that sRGB can accommodate most of the colors produced by a typical CMYK press.

Calibrating your display

Various software utilities are available that can guide you through adjusting your display. The operating system for your computer may come with such a utility. However, calibrating with software only isn't reliable. Human color perception automatically adapts color perception based on the colors the eyes are viewing, so they can't reliably make color decisions that are objective and precise.

To precisely calibrate your display for a professional graphics workflow, use a hardware color calibrator. This type of device has a sensor that you place on your display and software that will send color signals through your display. The sensor sees the color your display produces and determines the difference between the color it was supposed to produce and the color it actually produced. It uses this information to generate a profile about the display.

When you calibrate your display, you have to specify target values or aim points for the calibration. These values, such as the color temperature and gamma values, should be determined by your workflow. If you're not sure which ones to use, the default values are likely to be acceptable for web design, but for best results on CMYK print jobs consult with your prepress service provider for the display calibration target values it recommends.

Understanding different types of color profiles

● **Note:** It's important to realize that one profile cannot solve all of your color issues. What you need are profiles that accurately represent the color characteristics of each part of your workflow.

The aspect of color management you'll probably encounter most often is the *color profile*—a document that describes a color space, such as one of the following:

- **Capture profile.** This describes the color space of a device used to create an image, such as a camera or scanner. It can also be the color space first embedded into a document, such as for a digital painting.

- **Display profile.** This describes the color space of the screen or a computer or mobile device, and it's generated when you calibrate your monitor.

- **Document profile.** This describes the color space used by a file, such as a Photoshop image or an InDesign publication.

- **Output profile.** This describes the color space of where your work is viewed in the end. Although that could be a particular ink and paper combination on press, it can also be the profile of a specific device display or television standard.

- **Working space.** A working space is simply the default color space for an application. For example, if you set the working space of Photoshop to Adobe RGB, that will be the color space that's assumed when you open an image that doesn't already have a document profile. For more information, see the section "Choosing a Color Settings Preset."

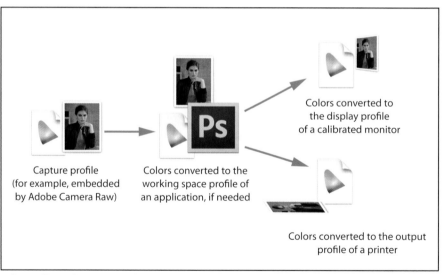

Color profiles make it possible for a color management system to keep color as consistent as possible among the parts of an Adobe Creative Suite workflow.

Having accurate profiles is critical because the color management system refers to them to find out about the color characteristics of each part of your workflow. For example, to display image colors accurately onscreen, the color management system uses the document color profile as a reference for colors in an image and uses the display profile to understand the range of colors that your display can reproduce. By comparing both of those color spaces, color management can help your display reproduce image colors to the best of its ability.

Choosing a Color Settings Preset

Some Adobe Creative Suite applications have a Color Settings command that displays a Color Settings dialog box. This dialog box is where you set an application's working space and specify how the application responds to documents with color profiles that are missing or don't match the working space (which you'll examine later). Although there are many settings in the Color Settings dialog box, Adobe provides Color Settings presets that set all the options at once. Adobe designed the presets to correspond to common workflows, and they're named accordingly. You'll choose a color preset that's appropriate for the upcoming lessons.

Tip: You can create custom Color Settings by changing the settings and clicking Save. If someone provides you with a custom Color Settings file, you can add those settings by clicking Load.

1   Start Adobe Photoshop CS6, and choose Edit > Color Settings.

2   In the Settings menu, try different Color Settings presets by choosing them from the Settings menu. Note that as you do this, multiple options may change. If your workflow is represented by one of the presets in the Settings menu, you only have to choose it there—you don't necessarily have to go through each option in the dialog box.

Tip: If you are working with prepress service providers outside North America, such as in Europe or Japan, you can display more international color presets in the Color Settings menu if you first click More Options.

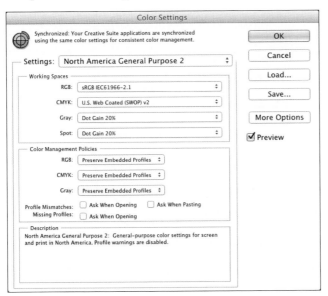

3 When you're done, make sure North America General Purpose 2 is selected in the Settings menu. You'll use this for the next lesson.

4 Click OK.

Tip: If you use some Adobe Creative Suite applications for print and others for the web, you might not want to synchronize their Color Settings for the same workflow.

You don't necessarily need to set Color Settings manually for multiple Adobe Creative Suite applications. Adobe Bridge contains a Creative Suite Color Settings command, providing you with a single location where you can choose a Color Settings preset that is then applied to Adobe Creative Suite applications that have a Color Settings command.

1 Start Adobe Bridge, and choose Edit > Creative Suite Color Settings.

2 If you see the word Synchronized at the top of the Suite Color Settings dialog box and North America General Purpose 2 is selected, click Cancel. Otherwise, select North America General Purpose 2 and click Apply.

Tip: If you are working with prepress service providers outside North America, such as in Europe or Japan, you can display more international presets in the Color Settings menu if you first select Show Expanded List of Color Settings Files.

Converting to, Assigning, and Embedding Profiles

Some Adobe Creative Suite applications contain commands that let you assign a color profile to an image or document, convert a document's colors to a different profile, or embed a profile into a document.

When no profile is assigned to a document, applications don't immediately know what range of colors the document uses, which can lead to incorrect color reproduction. Embedding a profile in a document lets applications know which color space a document uses by attaching a profile that describes its color space.

Converting colors is useful for times when your workflow requires that you provide a document in a specific color space. For example, you can use the Convert to Profile command if you have an image in RGB color mode and your job requires that it be handed off in the specific CMYK color space of your press. Similarly, you may want to take a ProPhoto RGB image produced by Adobe Camera Raw and convert it to sRGB for use on a website.

Next, you'll assign a corrected profile and embed it in the document.

1   Start Adobe Bridge, and make sure the Essentials workspace is selected at the top of the Adobe Bridge window.

2   Navigate to the Lesson09 folder on your hard drive, Shift-click the files Untagged.psd and Tagged.psd to select them both, and press Enter/Return to open them in Photoshop.

▶ **Tip:** When a document contains an embedded profile, you can think of "color space" and "color profile" as interchangeable terms, because a document's color space is described by its color profile.

3 In Photoshop choose Window > Arrange > 2-Up Vertical to display the images in two tabs side by side.

4 Select the Hand tool in the toolbar (or press H on the keyboard). Three color samplers appear in the active document.

Both images include three color samplers that you can monitor in the Info panel.

▶ **Tip:** Assigning the correct profile restores the intended appearance of an image without changing its color values. Converting colors to a different profile translates color values to another color space while preserving image appearance as much as possible.

The colors in the two images are different. Tagged.psd looks OK, but Untagged.psd appears to be color-shifted and unsaturated. You'll be able to compare the actual color values in both documents because they contain three color samplers over the door, the model's face, and one of the green lapels. However, you'll see the color samplers only in the active document.

5 If the Info panel isn't visible, choose Window > Info. It displays the color values for samplers #1, #2, and #3 in the active document. You may want to position the Info panel so that it doesn't cover up too much of the model.

6 Click the other document's tab to make it active. The color values in the Info panel don't change. You can switch between the two documents a few times to see that even though the color values are identical in the same locations in both documents, the image colors look different. The cause of the difference is not because the color values are wrong.

▶ **Tip:** Embedding a profile is also called *tagging*, so a document that's doesn't have an embedded profile is often called *untagged*.

7 Click the triangle to the right of the status bar and choose Document Profile from the menu that appears. Do the same in the other document tab. Setting Photoshop to display the document profiles reveals that they aren't using the same profile. In fact, Untagged.psd doesn't even have a profile embedded inside it. This means that even though the color values are the same, those values are being interpreted differently for each image.

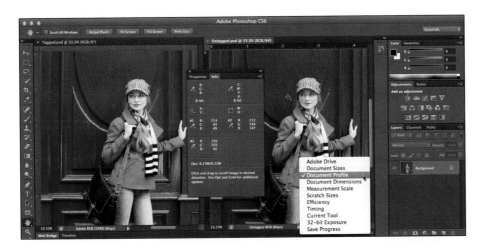

8 Choose Edit > Color Settings.

Tip: Another way to inspect embedded profiles is to look at the Metadata panel in Adobe Bridge as each document is selected.

In the Color Settings dialog box, the RGB working space is set to sRGB. This means that if an image has no profile, like the image Untagged.psd, Photoshop can only interpret its colors as if they're in the working space (because a working space is a default color space). Because the colors in Untagged.psd don't look right, you can guess that its actual color space is probably not sRGB. But which color space is it then? There are a couple of ways to figure this out.

The status bar for Tagged.psd shows Adobe RGB. That means Photoshop will interpret that document's colors as Adobe RGB regardless of the working space. In other words, because a profile is embedded in Tagged.psd, color-managed applications can always interpret its colors correctly. What happens if the working space is changed to Adobe RGB? Let's try that.

9 Choose Adobe RGB (1998) from the RGB menu in the Working Spaces section, and select the Preview check box to temporarily apply the change to all open documents. Untagged.psd does seem to match now.

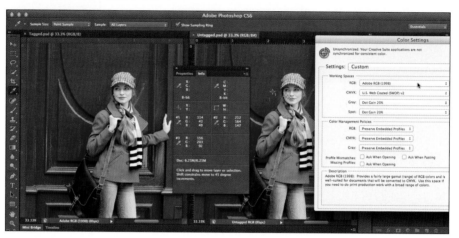

10 Click Cancel. Now you'll try a different method that will affect only the Untagged.psd document instead of altering the Color Settings for the entire application.

11 Make sure Untagged.psd is active, and choose Edit > Assign Profile. If you see a warning about the appearance of layers, click OK.

The Assign Profile dialog box is currently set to Don't Color Manage This Document. If the document had a profile, selecting that option would remove it.

12 Select the second option, Working RGB: sRGB IEC61966-2.1. This doesn't change the appearance of the image; because the document has no embedded profile, its colors are already being interpreted using the working space and it isn't correct.

13 Select the third option, Profile. This lets you apply any profile that's installed. Although the list of profiles may be very long, you should first try each profile in the group of five standard profiles near the top of the menu. These are installed with Adobe Creative Suite.

You should find that choosing Adobe RGB (1998) produces colors that are the most plausible. It's a safe bet that Adobe RGB (1998) was the color space last used to edit this image.

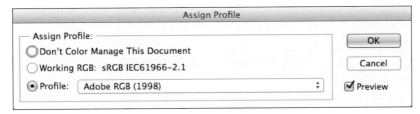

14 Click OK. Adobe RGB (1998) is now the profile applied to Untagged.psd.

15 Choose File > Save. Now the ProPhoto RGB profile is embedded in the document. You can verify this by checking the status bar.

16 Close Tagged.psd.

Untagged.psd now contains a correct embedded profile, which means its colors will be interpreted as intended in other color-managed applications, such as Adobe InDesign. However, in a scenario where this image is made available to the general public, there will be no guarantee that it will always be used in applications that can properly use an Adobe RGB (1998) profile. (While Adobe RGB (1998) is often used in graphic design workflows, it is not common in the general computer market.) To maximize the chance that the colors will appear correct on most computers, you'll convert a copy of the document to the sRGB color space. The reason is that devices, displays, and printers that aren't color managed are at least manufactured to approximate the sRGB color space.

17 With Untagged.psd active, choose Image > Duplicate.

18 In the Duplicate Image dialog box, enter **For Media Use**, and click OK.

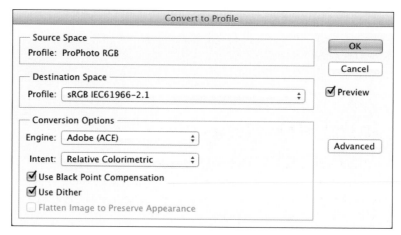

Duplicating is a good idea if you want to preserve the original document, especially in a case like this where you'll convert from a larger color space to a much smaller one.

19 Choose Edit > Convert to Profile, and in the Profile menu for Destination Space, choose sRGB IEC61966-2.1. You can see that the Convert to Profile dialog box clearly shows you the source and destination color spaces for the conversion.

20 Click OK, and notice that the status bar updates with the new color space.

21 Choose File > Save. Accept the suggested filename and make sure the Lesson09 folder is the current folder.

Notice that Embed Color Profile is selected. The current document profile will be included with the image.

22 Click Save.

23 Close all of the documents, saving changes when asked.

You'll find that Adobe Illustrator and Adobe InDesign have similar Color Settings, Assign Profile, and Convert to Profile commands so that you can fully color manage their documents as well.

Locating and installing color profiles

When you acquire new devices, inks, papers, or software, you don't necessarily have to know how to install color profiles. For example, when you install Adobe Creative Suite, it automatically installs the profiles it needs. When you calibrate your display, the calibration software automatically installs the profile it generates. Profiles are also typically installed when you run the installer utility for a color printer.

On Mac OS X, profiles are installed at *[hard drive name]/Library/ColorSync/Profiles*. You can manually drag profiles into that folder, which you may do after you download profiles from the web. In some cases, they might be installed within your home folder in [username]/*Library/ColorSync/Profiles*. If they're installed in the latter location, they're only visible when you're logged into your account. Also note that in Mac OS X 10.7 and later, the Library folder in your home folder is hidden by default, but you can reveal it in the Finder by holding down the Option key and choosing Go/Library.

On Windows 7, profiles are installed at *\Windows\system32\spool\drivers\color*. You can install a profile by simply double-clicking it.

Setting Up a Color-managed Print Workflow

Because there are several significantly different print technologies that are commonly used, multiple print workflows require different approaches to color management. In this lesson, you'll set up two common print workflows: printing on a desktop inkjet printer and printing on a press.

At first glance it may seem that both desktop printers and printing presses reproduce color with CMYK inks, but most inkjet printers are actually designed to receive RGB data, which means it's best to use images and a workflow that are RGB-based.

Traditional prepress workflows are designed to receive CMYK data, so in that case you'd use images and workflows that are CMYK-based. But keep in mind that some newer prepress workflows also accept RGB images and can convert them to CMYK automatically. As always, consult with your prepress service provider to verify that your workflow is appropriate for your output.

▶ **Tip:** If you use AdobeRGB or ProPhoto RGB as a working space so that you can use a wider range of colors, editing 16 bit/channel images helps ensure higher-quality results than editing 8 bit/channel images.

Working with an RGB-based print workflow in InDesign

RGB-based print workflows include most desktop color printers. The driver software for these printers expects RGB data, and the default for many printers is to expect sRGB data. You'll try the simpler sRGB workflow first, and then you'll try an advanced workflow that is more likely to take advantage of all the colors in a printer.

1   In your Lesson09 folder in Adobe Bridge, double-click the file Local.indd. This is a one-page promotional poster for a magazine.

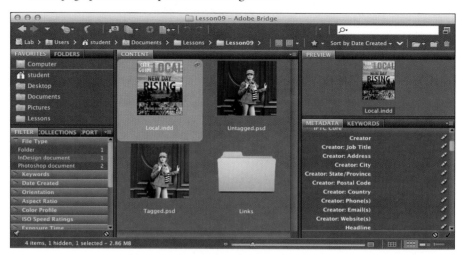

Note: If a Policy or Profile Mismatch warning appears when you open the InDesign document, select Leave As Is and click OK. You may see the warning twice, for RGB and CMYK color.

2   In InDesign, make sure the Essentials workspace is selected, and then choose Reset Essentials from the workspace menu on the Application Bar to make sure the workspace is restored to its default settings.

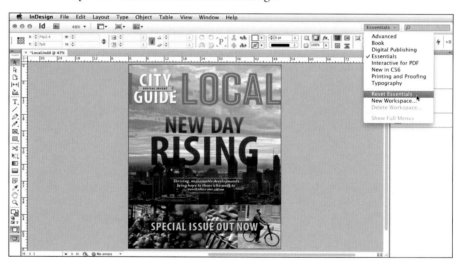

3   Click the Links panel to open it. This document contains five images.

4 Choose Panel Options from the Links panel menu.

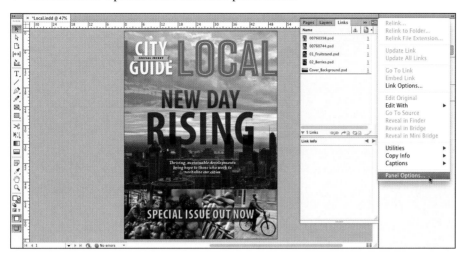

5 In the Panel Options dialog box under Show Column, select the options Color Space and ICC Profile. Then click OK.

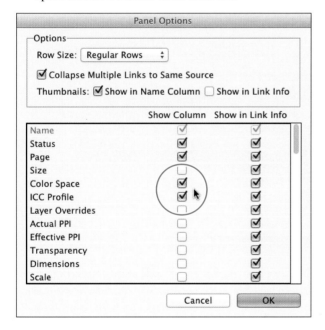

6   Drag any edge of the Links panel to make it wider. Now you can view the color management status of every image at a glance.

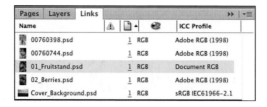

One of the images, 01_Fruitstand.psd, is listed as Document RGB under the ICC Profile column. That image should have an embedded Adobe RGB profile in it, but it's currently using the document default because it's untagged. You can assign a profile to an image using InDesign.

7   Click the underlined number 1 under the page column for 01_Fruitstand.psd. This selects the image where it's located on page 1.

8   Choose Object > Image Color Settings, and for Profile, choose Adobe RGB (1998). Then click OK.

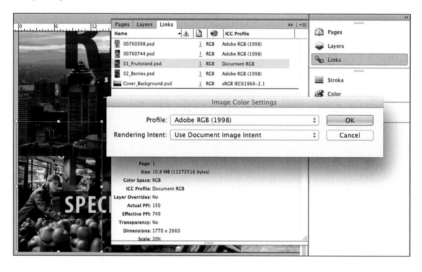

The Image Color Settings dialog box lets you assign a profile and a rendering intent to any image in InDesign. This can save you time because you don't have to go all the way back to Photoshop to resave images with the correct embedded profiles. However, keep in mind that the changes you make with Image Color Settings affect only the selected instance of the image in InDesign, not the original image.

Now the Links panel indicates that you've overridden the image file's profile setting.

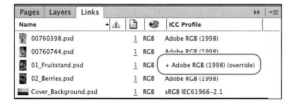

9 Choose File > Print. This part of the lesson requires that an RGB-based printer be installed; any color office printer or photo printer should be satisfactory.

10 Select the Color Management pane.

By default, the Print section is set to use the document profile as the source color space for output. If needed, you can then convert those colors, and the colors of all images, to another color space in the Options section.

11 To set the Printer Profile option correctly, be aware of the level of print quality you're aiming for:

• For general office printing or to print on devices that don't provide specialized color profiles, set Printer Profile to sRGB IEC61966-2.1. In this lesson, the Local publication document profile is already set to sRGB and the InDesign working space is also sRGB, so you can choose either Document RGB or Working RGB. If neither was already set to sRGB, you'd be able to choose the sRGB profile further down in the menu.

- For color-critical printing on high-end photo or fine-art printers where profiles are supplied for the printer and for ink and paper combinations, choose the profile that represents the printing conditions. Those profiles are listed alphabetically in the lower part of the Printer Profile menu. When you do this, also click the Printer button at the bottom of the Print dialog box and disable color management in the printer driver so that colors are not double converted. The exact steps for disabling color management in the printer driver are not covered here because they vary depending on the type of printer and the versions of the operating system and printer driver.

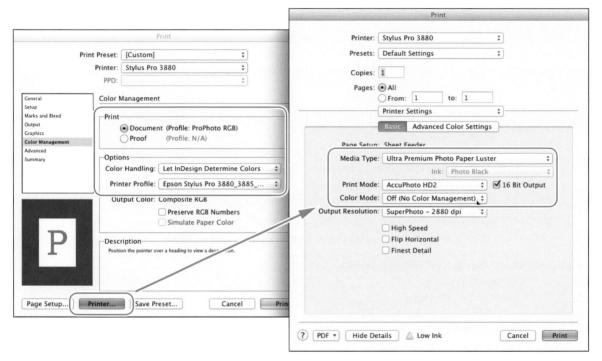

For color-critical RGB printing in InDesign, select the correct Printer Profile in the Color Management pane (left), and also turn off color management in the printer driver settings (right) to avoid double correction. Your printer driver settings may not match the software used in this example.

12 At this point you can click Print or click Cancel.

Working with a CMYK-based print workflow in InDesign

Preparing a print job for a CMYK workflow is similar to the RGB workflow you just tried, but potentially with some important differences.

1 In InDesign, choose Edit > Color Settings, and choose North America Prepress 2. This preset switches the RGB working space to Adobe RGB and turns on profile mismatch and missing profile warnings so that you're alerted to any files that differ from these Color Settings.

The InDesign Color Settings dialog box has a CMYK Color Management Policy that isn't in Photoshop: Preserve Numbers (Ignore Linked Profiles). This is provided for CMYK workflows where the images have already been converted into the correct CMYK color space and the current color values in those images must be preserved. This accommodates some traditional CMYK workflows. Consult your prepress service provider to confirm which color management policy to use.

2 Click OK.

You may remember (or see in the Links panel) that the images in this document are in RGB color mode. If this was an older, traditional CMYK workflow, you would want to bring all of those images back into Photoshop and use the Convert to Profile command to convert them to the exact CMYK color space of the specific press in use. In newer workflows, the conversion to CMYK can be left to InDesign or the prepress output device, so the images can be left in RGB color mode in InDesign. For this lesson, we'll assume the conversion will be done by InDesign.

The next few steps describe how to create a PDF/X-1a document, because PDF is an increasingly common interchange format for handing off prepress jobs. Your prepress service provider may require a different PDF/X format or may ask for your native InDesign files and links so that it can print from them directly; as always, you should verify your workflow with your prepress service provider.

3   Choose File > Export, choose Adobe PDF (Print) from the Format menu, and click Save. This opens the Export Adobe PDF dialog box.

4   For Adobe PDF Preset, choose PDF/X-1a:2001. This is one variation of the common PDF/X standard and will produce a PDF file that conforms to the requirements for a high-end prepress. Your prepress service provider may recommend a different preset.

5   Click Output. The Output pane controls the color conversion to CMYK and contains options similar to those you saw in the Print dialog box. You don't have to change anything here because the preset you chose makes all of the options consistent with the PDF/X-1a standard.

In many cases you won't have to adjust the Output panel, because if your prepress service provider requires a variation from these settings, it may provide you with a customized Adobe PDF Preset that you can install and choose just like this one.

6   Click Export. The PDF file is created and is ready to hand off.

7   Close the Local.indd document. Save changes if asked.

The process in Adobe Illustrator is very similar except that you create a PDF file by choosing File > Save As instead of through an Export command.

Controlling color printing in Photoshop

The color printing process in Photoshop is similar to InDesign and Illustrator but has a little more control over sizing and previewing.

Before you spend time and money making test prints, you can preview how your colors will output using a feature called *soft-proofing*. It uses printer and monitor profiles to simulate the conversions that your document colors will undergo.

1 In your Lesson09 folder in Adobe Bridge, double-click the file Tagged.psd.

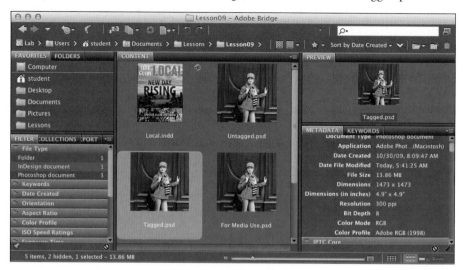

2 Choose View > Proof Setup > Working CMYK. The Proof Setup submenu contains commands that simulate various output scenarios.

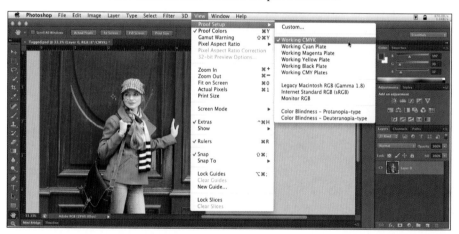

> **Tip:** When the Proof Colors command is turned on, in addition to seeing the results in the document window, you can also see the proofed color values in the Info panel. They appear next to the original color values.

Choosing Working CMYK applies your current CMYK working space profile to the display to simulate how the image colors will print in CMYK; doing this also selects the View > Proof Colors command. To help indicate that you are viewing an output simulation, the text CMYK is added to the document's tab title.

3 Choose View > Proof Setup > Custom. This dialog box shows you how soft-proofing is currently set up. For a more accurate simulation, select the Simulate Paper Color option (this will automatically select the Simulate Black Ink option), and then click OK.

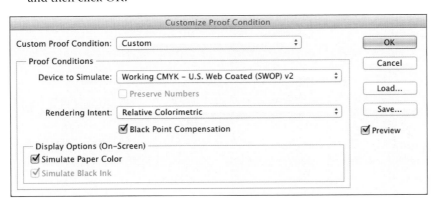

The image appears to lose contrast, and some colors are significantly less saturated. This is expected, because CMYK output cannot reproduce the same range of colors and tones as a computer display. A soft-proofing preview helps you make corrections with a visual reference to the final output conditions.

4 Press Ctrl-Y/Command-Y. This is the shortcut for the View > Proof Colors command, and lets you quickly compare the soft-proof to the unproofed image.

5 Choose Window > Arrange > New Window for Tagged.psd, and then choose Window > Arrange > 2-Up Vertical. This is not a duplicate of the file but a second view of the same file.

6 Make sure View > Proof Colors is turned off for one view and turned on for the other view. This lets you check the unproofed image and the soft-proof view side by side.

7 Choose File > Print. The options in the Color Management section are similar to those you saw in InDesign. The Match Print Colors and Show Paper White options soft-proof the image in the same way as the Proof Colors command.

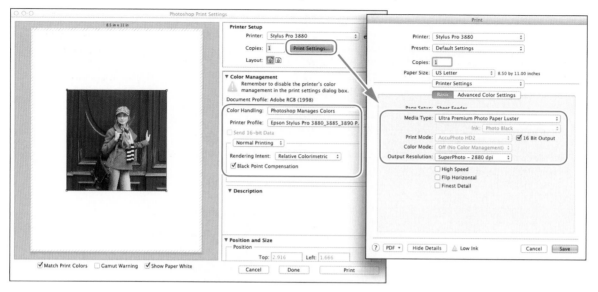

For color-critical RGB printing in Photoshop, select the correct Printer Profile in the Color Management pane (left), and also make sure color management is turned off in the printer driver settings (right) to avoid double correction. Your printer driver settings may not match this example.

8 Scroll down to show the Position and Size section.

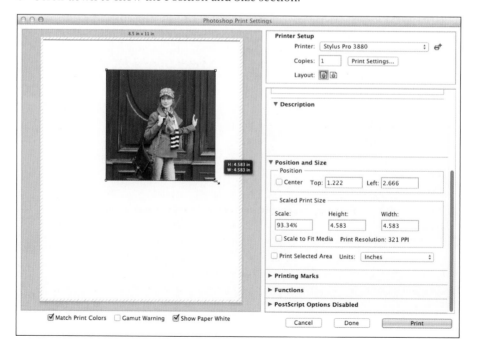

In this section you can control the placement, scale, and resolution of the printed image to a greater degree than in other Adobe Creative Suite software.

9   Feel free to explore the Position and Size options:

- To reposition the image, simply drag the image or edit the Top and Left position values.

- To change the size of the image, enter a Scale, Height, or Width, or select Scale to Fit Media. If you change these values, the Print Resolution must change because the number of pixels is locked. If you want to resize with control over resolution, click Done and choose Image > Image Size; this will let you use the Resample option to control resolution.

10 If you are connected to the printer you were specifying settings for, you can click Print. Otherwise, click Done.

● **Note:** The PostScript Options at the bottom of the Print dialog box are available only when you print to a PostScript-language output device.

Understanding color management policies

Color-managed applications use profiles to determine how to handle the colors in your documents. What should happen when you open documents that don't match the profiles set for an application? That's where color management policies come in. Located in the bottom half of the Color Settings dialog box, color management policies in Adobe Creative Suite applications typically include the following sets of options:

- A menu where you tell the application what to do when a document you open has an embedded profile that's different than the application's working space. You can choose Off (leave the incoming document alone), Preserve Embedded Profiles (usually a safe choice), or Convert to Working Space (for specialized workflows). You can set this for each output color mode that the application supports; for instance, you can have the application handle RGB documents differently than CMYK documents.

- Profile Mismatches check boxes that let you specify when the application should let you know that a document you're opening uses a color space that's different than the application's working space.

- A Missing Profiles check box that let you specify when the application should inform you that you're opening a document without an embedded profile.

If you need to keep a close eye on each document's color space, select the Profile Mismatches and Missing Profiles options. However, keep in mind that if these options are on and you work with a large number of documents with differing color spaces or missing profiles, selecting these check boxes may result in many alerts.

If you're new to color management, the number of options for color management policies may seem overwhelming. The easiest way to set all the options at once is to choose a Color Settings preset; see "Setting Up a Color-managed Print Workflow" and "Setting Up Web Color Workflow" in this lesson

Choosing a rendering intent

Color-managed applications in Adobe Creative Suite may have a Rendering Intent option, which gives you additional control when you convert colors from a larger color space to a smaller one. Rendering intents can come into play not only when using the Convert to Profile command, but also when soft-proofing and printing, because those actions also convert between color spaces. The names of the rendering intents can be intimidating, but when it comes down to making a choice, it's actually very simple. Technically, the four choices have the following meanings:

- **Perceptual** scales a larger color space (such as Adobe RGB) into a smaller one (such as sRGB). The advantage is that color relationships are preserved, but the disadvantage is that color values may be altered.

- **Relative Colorimetric** simply eliminates any color values of a larger color space that are outside a smaller color space. The advantage is that color values aren't changed, but the disadvantage is that colors may lose visible detail if their original color values were outside the smaller color space.

- **Absolute Colorimetric** is like Relative Colorimetric except that it adjusts the white point color value when preserving the color of the original paper is desired. You probably won't use this very much unless you're printing hard proofs.

- **Saturation** scales the larger color space to the smaller one like Perceptual does but maps fully saturated colors to the maximum color values possible in the smaller color space. It can be used for images in which you want to emphasize bright colors, although it's used more for line art than for photographs.

When you choose a rendering intent, in most cases you'll choose between Perceptual and Relative Colorimetric because the other two are less commonly used. It isn't easy to predict which rendering intent will work better for a particular image, so if color is critical, you should test it both ways; consider soft-proofing so that you can try both onscreen. If you're converting between color spaces that are similar in size and shape, the difference between Perceptual and Relative Colorimetric may not be significant.

Setting Up a Web Color Workflow

Although color management is valuable in achieving consistent color in print, it's a larger challenge on the web because most computers on the web are not color managed. The best you can do is aim for a generic standard that may be approximated by most computers. The sRGB color space was designed to be such a standard, so it's reasonable to use sRGB as the basis for a web design workflow. You'll convert the colors of a photo for web use.

1   With the file Tagged.psd still open in Photoshop, click the tab that you were using to view soft-proofing, and choose View > Proof Setup > Internet Standard RGB (sRGB). Now you're no longer proofing to CMYK but to web colors.

2   Choose Edit > Color Settings.

3   In the Settings menu, choose North America Web/Internet.

Notice that this sets the RGB working space to sRGB and sets the color management policies to convert RGB images to the working space (sRGB).

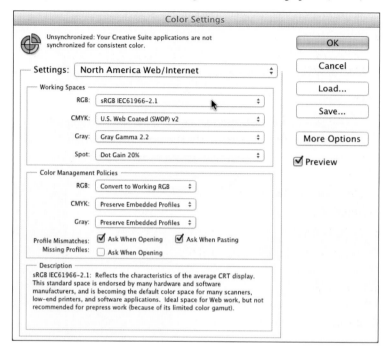

4 Click OK.

5 Choose File > Save for Web.

6 If your display doesn't match the following figure, click the 2-Up tab.

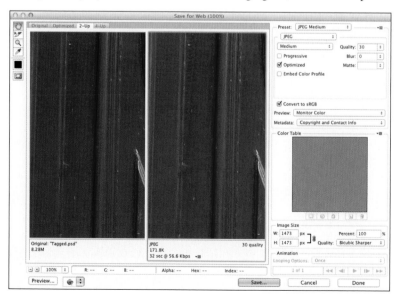

7 The current image size is too large for a web page, so in the Image Size section enter **400** for W (width) and press the Tab key to apply it; then choose Bicubic Sharper from the Quality menu in the same Image Size options group.

8 Click the left image. It's labeled Original at the bottom. Now click the right image, and note that the options in the Presets section change to indicate the settings applied to the preview of the optimized image.

9 Do the following to optimize image quality and color for the web:

• From the Preset menu in the top-right corner of the Save for Web dialog box, choose JPEG High. You can change this setting depending on your requirements for quality and file size, which you can evaluate at the bottom of the right image.

• Make sure Embed Color Profile is not selected. The reason is that non-image web page content is not color managed, so using a profile may make it difficult to match image colors with other web page elements.

• Make sure that Convert to sRGB is selected. The original image uses the Adobe RGB color space, which will not be interpreted properly in non-color-managed web browsers and applications. This is why the Original view on the left doesn't look as good in this preview, and why the image on the right looks better when you select Convert to sRGB.

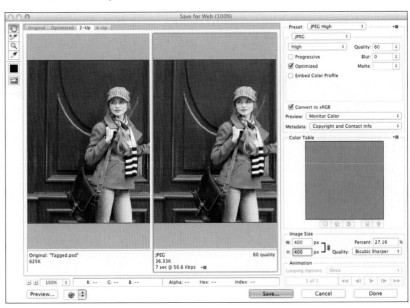

10 Click Save. In the Save Optimized As dialog box, leave the default settings, navigate to your Lesson09 folder, and click the Save button here too. If you want, you can drag the exported JPEG image to a web browser to see how it turned out. If you see a warning about filename characters, click OK to continue.

Color management on web browsers and mobile devices

Some web browsers are color managed; they can use your operating system's color management feature to properly interpret images that contain embedded color profiles. However, some browsers that do support color management don't have it turned on by default. In addition, some browsers color manage images but not other parts of a web page, such as colors in HTML layers. Also, some popular image formats used on web pages don't support ICC profiles, such as GIF. And finally, even if an image with an embedded profile does display in a color-managed browser, chances are viewers' monitors have not been accurately calibrated unless the viewers are graphics professionals.

At the time this book is being written, color handling on mobile devices is much like it is for the web: ICC profiles are not consistently supported. Accordingly, the current strategy for color on mobile devices is essentially the same as for the web: Use sRGB as the working space and the color space to which you export images.

Adobe Flash does provide for color management, but it's limited. For more information, see www.adobe.com/devnet/flash/quickstart/color_correction_as3.html.

Resolving Color Space Mismatches

When you open a document that uses a color space that is different than the application's working space, you may see a warning. What do you do when you see this type of alert? You're given the following choices:

- **Use the embedded profile (instead of the working space).** Choose this if you're sure the embedded profile is correct. The application will represent the document's color as it was in the application that last saved it.

- **Convert document's colors to the working space.** Choose this if your working space is set properly for your workflow, and your workflow requires that all documents be converted to the working space. The document's color values will be converted, but its color appearance will be preserved as much as possible—although the appearance may change if it's converted between significantly different color spaces.

- **Discard the embedded profile (don't color manage).** Choose this if your workflow requires that documents not have profiles embedded in them. The document's appearance won't change if its color space already matches your working space. If the two color spaces don't match, the document's appearance will probably change.

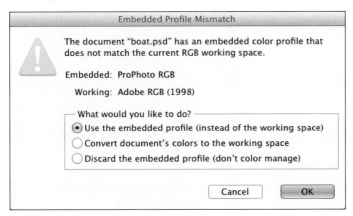

In the case of a missing profile alert, you should assign a profile only if you're sure it accurately represents the color space of the document. If you're not sure, simply continue opening the document without assigning a profile (the Don't Color Manage option) so that you can use the Assign Profile command in Photoshop or the Image Color Settings command in InDesign to try out profiles while previewing them to make sure you're assigning the correct one.

Wrapping Up

If you're still learning about color management and aren't sure if your system and applications are set up correctly for color management, a safe route in the meantime is to use sRGB as a working space and an output space. Using sRGB minimizes the amount of manual conversion you'll need to do with files you import or export. sRGB is also recommended for web workflows.

If you're designing for print or for workflows where high output quality is a priority, over the long term your goal should be to understand how to use color spaces and color profiles, how to soft-proof in the Adobe Creative Suite applications that support it, and how to convert between color profiles. Remember that you can use soft-proofing to check your colors against your output conditions before you commit to expensive and time-consuming output.

Review questions

1 What's the difference between a color mode and a color space?

2 What is a color profile and what does it do?

3 What are the five types of color profiles you may encounter?

4 What's the difference between assigning a profile and converting to a profile?

5 Why is it difficult to use color profiles on the web and on mobile devices, and what's a realistic strategy for handling image color on the web?

Review answers

1 A color mode is a method of representing color, such as RGB or CMYK. A color space is a specific range of colors, such as the range that a device can reproduce.

2 A color profile is a document that records or describes a color space so that applications can make accurate color conversions between color spaces.

3 You may encounter a capture profile, a display profile, a document profile, an output profile, and a working space profile.

4 Assigning a profile simply associates a profile with a document to restore its intended appearance by interpreting its color values, which don't change. Converting to a different profile does change color values, but the appearance of the image changes as little as possible.

5 Not all web browsers or mobile devices are color-managed, and few computer monitors are properly calibrated. But many devices, displays, and printers are manufactured to be somewhat close to the sRGB color space, so sRGB is a relatively good color space for online or mobile work.

INDEX

grid layouts for multiple photos, 88–90
grouping objects for export, 122, 124
Guide-based Liquid Layout rule, 141

H

halftone cells, 224
handheld devices. *See* mobile devices
help resources, 3–4
hiding. *See* showing/hiding
hosting reviews
    initiating shared reviews, 212
    online web conferences, 213–218
HSB color mode, 225, 253
HTML
    exporting HTML pages from Fireworks,
        163–164
    saving files in Dreamweaver, 154
hyperlinks
    buttons vs., 137, 149
    creating, 135–136
    function of, 135

I

Identity Setup dialog box, 204
Illustrator CS6, 27–47
    adjusting quality of saved
        graphics, 47
    converting bitmap to vector graphics,
        28–31
    creating patterns, 31–32
    cutting and pasting art on
        artboards, 42
    drawing in perspective, 43–46
    editing and applying patterns
        in, 34–35
    overview, 11, 27
    refining vector graphics with Blob Brush,
        38–40

tool bar for, 38
using Bristle Brush for vector graphics,
    35–38
using Image Trace, 25, 28–35
vector graphics used in, 27
working with multiple artboards, 40–43
Illustrator Options dialog box, 47
Image Color Settings dialog box, 266
Image Import Options dialog box, 73
Image Trace, 25, 28–35
images. *See also* graphics; preparing images;
    raw images
    assigning profile and rendering intent
        for, 266
    backgrounds removed from, 54–57
    converting to vector graphics, 25
    cropping, 48–51, 234–236
    displaying dimensions in status bar, 242
    editing tools for, 15
    file formats for master, 222
    generating captions from metadata,
        90–91
    inspecting edited, 230–231, 237
    laying out in grid, 88–90
    optimizing quality and color for web,
        279
    poster, 139, 149
    preparing for multiple media, 222
    preparing for print, 239–243
    removing objects from, 57–59
    reviewing, 244–247
    scaling, 107, 224
    selecting from overlapping frames,
        71–72
    sharpening and cropping Photoshop,
        234–236
    verifying resolution of linked, 97–98
    working with raw, 76–81
importing
    PSD files into InDesign, 243

smartphones. *See also* mobile devices
about, 106
previewing website on, 157–159
soft-proofing, 271
Spot Healing Brush, 59, 60–61
spring-loaded cursors, 92, 93
Sticky Note Properties dialog box, 208
Style Mapping dialog box, 82–83
styling text, 83
subtractive color, 252
Suite Color Settings dialog box, 26, 256
SVG (Scalable Vector Graphics) file format, 233
synchronizing color settings, 26, 252, 255–256

T

tablets. *See also* iPad apps
about, 106
preparing high-resolution displays for, 233
previewing website on, 157–159
understanding resolution of, 223
tagging profiles, 258
Tap To View Controller option (Folio Overlays panel), 139
templates
creating document from jQuery Mobile, 108–111
customizing InDesign, 68
using and modifying InDesign CS6, 68
testing
interactive overlays, 140, 149
layouts in Adobe Content Viewer, 149
page orientation changes, 143
text
adding sidebars on layers, 88
aligning headings on PDF forms, 194–196

applying paragraph styles, 84–85
importing and styling, 82–83
resizing in text fields, 187
reviewing and marking up, 209
splitting within and across columns, 86–88
tracking changes in InDesign, 93–95
using web fonts for, 233
wrapping around frames, 85–86
text fields
adding in InDesign form, 184–188
adding in PDF forms, 183–188
automatically resizing text in, 187
changing attributes for, 188
uses for, 188
Text Frame Options dialog box, 87
Text Wrap panel, 86
Tilt-Shift Blur, 10, 51–53
timeline adjustments for multiple layers, 130–133
Track Changes panel, 94–95
Tracker
about, 200, 210
comment management in Review panel, 202
illustrated, 210
initiating shared reviews from, 212
managing reviews with, 210–213
troubleshooting online meetings, 214

U

Unique ID for EPUBs, 128
untagged documents, 258
uploading files for collaborative reviews, 206
User dialog box, 94

Y

Z

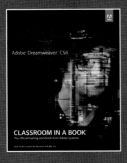

The fastest, easiest, most comprehensive way to learn
Adobe Creative Suite 6

Classroom in a Book®, the best-selling series of hands-on software training books, helps you learn the features of Adobe software quickly and easily.

The **Classroom in a Book** series offers what no other book or training program does—an official training series from Adobe Systems, developed with the support of Adobe product experts.

To see a complete list of our Adobe® Creative Suite® 6 titles go to
www.peachpit.com/adobecs6

Adobe Photoshop CS6 Classroom in a Book
ISBN: 9780321827333

Adobe Illustrator CS6 Classroom in a Book
ISBN: 9780321822482

Adobe InDesign CS6 Classroom in a Book
ISBN: 9780321822499

Adobe Flash Professional CS6 Classroom in a Book
ISBN: 9780321822512

Adobe Dreamweaver CS6 Classroom in a Book
ISBN: 9780321822451

Adobe Muse Classroom in a Book
ISBN: 9780321821362

Adobe Fireworks CS6 Classroom in a Book
ISBN: 9780321822444

Adobe Premiere Pro CS6 Classroom in a Book
ISBN: 9780321822475

Adobe After Effects CS6 Classroom in a Book
ISBN: 9780321822437

Adobe Audition CS6 Classroom in a Book
ISBN: 9780321832832

Adobe Creative Suite 6 Design & Web Premium Classroom in a Book
ISBN: 9780321822604

Adobe Creative Suite 6 Production Premium Classroom in a Book
ISBN: 9780321832689

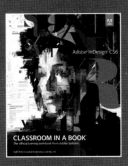

Adobe**Press**

AdobePress

LEARN BY VIDEO

The **Learn by Video** series from video2brain and Adobe Press is the only Adobe-approved video courseware for the Adobe Certified Associate Level certification, and has quickly established itself as one of the most critically acclaimed training products available on the fundamentals of Adobe software.

Learn by Video offers up to 15 hours of high-quality HD video training presented by experienced trainers, as well as lesson files, assessment quizzes, and review materials. The DVD is bundled with a full-color printed booklet that provides supplemental information as well as a guide to the video topics.

Table of Contents never more than a click away

Up to 15 hours of high-quality video training

Lesson files are included on the DVD

Video player remembers which movie you watched last

Watch-and-Work mode shrinks the video into a small window while you work in the software

For more information go to
www.adobepress.com/learnbyvideo

Titles

Adobe Photoshop CS6: Learn by Video: Core Training in Visual Communication
ISBN: 9780321840714

Adobe Illustrator CS6: Learn by Video
ISBN: 9780321840684

Adobe InDesign CS6: Learn by Video
ISBN: 9780321840691

Adobe Flash Professional CS6: Learn by Video: Core Training in Rich Media Communication
ISBN: 9780321840707

Adobe Dreamweaver CS6: Learn by Video: Core Training in Web Communication
ISBN: 9780321840370

Adobe Premiere Pro CS6: Learn by Video: Core Training in Video Communication
ISBN: 9780321840721

Adobe After Effects CS6: Learn by Video
ISBN: 9780321840387

WATCH
READ
CREATE

Unlimited online access to all Peachpit, Adobe Press, Apple Training and New Riders videos and books, as well as content from other leading publishers including: O'Reilly Media, Focal Press, Sams, Que, Total Training, John Wiley & Sons, Course Technology PTR, Class on Demand, VTC and more.

No time commitment or contract required! Sign up for one month or a year.
All for $19.99 a month

SIGN UP TODAY
peachpit.com/creativeedge